ITEM

D1424762

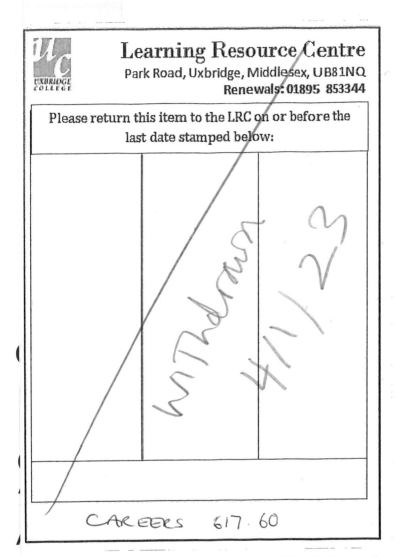

11th edition

trotman | **t**

Getting into guides

Getting into Art & Design Courses, 11th edition
Getting into Business & Economics Courses, 13th edition
Getting into Dental School, 11th edition
Getting into Engineering Courses, 5th edition
Getting into Law, 12th edition
Getting into Medical School: 2020 Entry, 24th edition
Getting into Oxford & Cambridge: 2020 Entry, 22nd edition
Getting into Pharmacy and Pharmacology Courses, 2nd edition
Getting into Physiotherapy Courses, 9th edition
Getting into Psychology Courses, 12th edition
Getting into Veterinary School, 11th edition
How to Complete Your UCAS Application: 2020 Entry, 31st edition

Getting into Dental School

This 11th edition published in 2019 by Trotman Education, an imprint of Crimson Publishing Ltd, 21d Charles Street, Bath BA1 1HX

© Crimson Publishing Ltd 2019

Author: Adam Cross

7th–10th edns: Adam Cross
6th edn: Steven Piumatti
5th edn: James Burnett
3rd & 4th edns: James Burnett & Andrew Long
2nd edn: Joe Ruston & James Burnett
1st edn: Joe Ruston
Editions 1–4 published by Trotman and Co. Ltd

British Library Cataloguing in Publication Data
A catalogue record of this book is available from the British Library.

ISBN: 978 1 912943 04 3

Printed and bound in Malta by Gutenberg Press Ltd

Contents

Contents

About the author

Adam Cross is Vice Principal at the independent college MPW Birmingham and has a number of years' expertise in helping students gain entry onto highly competitive undergraduate courses such as dentistry and medicine. In addition to his UCAS and careers guidance expertise, Adam also helps students with pre-admissions tests such as the University Clinical Aptitude Test (UCAT) and BioMedical Admissions Test (BMAT). Adam studied Biological Sciences at Lancaster University and currently teaches A level Biology at MPW.

Acknowledgements

I would like to thank all of the individuals who have given their time to provide information to me. In particular I would like to thank Yusra Khan, Simran Chahal, Jasdeep Johal, Anika Kanda, Utkarsh Dandekar, Karan Maini, Puja Jalota and Ayesha Mohammed, as well as numerous others, for giving me an insight into life as a dental student. I would also like to thank Dr Anthony Dash and Dr Kully Shoker for giving an insight into the world of dentistry. I would like to give a special mention to Dr Sameera Mukadam, who has given endless assistance and information to me about so many areas of the profession and has pestered countless dental students and dentists to provide me with case studies.

In addition, I would like to thank the admissions teams from all of the UK dental schools, the British Dental Association and the British Dental Health Foundation for providing material relating to the world of dentistry. Finally, I would like to thank my wife and family for their support while I was writing the book.

I would like to emphasise here that although the information in the book has been provided by experts, most of the views expressed are my own, and any mistakes are also mine.

Adam Cross

Introduction

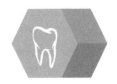

If you have picked up this book, you are probably considering applying to study dentistry and ultimately want to become a dentist. At this stage of the process, you may be unsure about the details of how to apply, or how best to prepare yourself for an admissions interview. You may have no idea about the type of work experience you will be required to have or the demands of pre-admissions tests. However, the whole purpose of this book is to provide you with a step-by-step guide to the whole process and ensure that you are prepared to make a successful application and secure your place at university.

This book is divided into the following chapters, which will guide you through each stage of the process.

Chapter 1 gives an overview of studying dentistry at university and describes the experiences you will have as an undergraduate and the key elements of the course structure. It then explores options for post-graduate study and the various specialisms that exist.

Chapter 2 outlines the importance of work experience and voluntary work when making your application and the areas for you to focus on to maximise your chances of successfully applying.

Chapter 3 includes advice on what to consider when choosing the course you wish to apply to. It looks in particular at what to consider when attending open days and the various academic requirements that the courses have.

Chapter 4 deals with preparing your application to make it as attractive as possible to admissions tutors. It includes advice on the UCAS application procedure and also deals with the University Clinical Aptitude Test (UCAT) and BioMedical Admissions Test (BMAT) and how best to prepare for them.

Chapter 5 focuses on the personal statement and how to write it. It looks at the general structure of the statement and the elements that need to be included to make you stand out.

Chapter 6 provides advice on how to prepare for multiple mini interviews (MMIs) and panel interviews. It also gives some examples of the types of questions that you may be asked. It goes on to provide key information on some current dental issues, such as mouth cancer, fluoridation of water and NHS dentistry.

Chapter 7 gives information about international students applying to study dentistry, but also deals with applications from other non-standard applicants, such as mature students, graduates, students who have studied arts A levels, and retake students.

Chapter 8 looks at the options you have on results day and describes the steps that you need to take if you miss the grades or do not hold any offers.

Chapter 9 looks at the financial elements of being a dental student and gives details of fees, student loans and grants across the UK.

Chapter 10 looks at career options in dentistry and the different pathways that a dentist could follow. It also looks at your graduate prospects as a dentist and what typical earnings are.

Finally, in **Chapter 11**, you can find details of all the dental schools and key dental organisations, plus a glossary that can be used to decipher any technical terms you come across.

There are a number of case studies provided throughout the book to support the material being discussed. This information is designed to illustrate the appropriate points and should give you an opportunity to see the issues under consideration demonstrated. Like other books in this series, such as *Getting into Medical School*, this title is designed to be a route map for potential dentists rather than a guide to dentistry as a profession. Further information on issues relating to being a dentist can be found on websites such as the British Dental Association's (the BDA – see www.bda.org), or directly from your own dentist.

Entrance requirements have been given primarily in terms of A level grades throughout the book; information for students who have studied Scottish Highers, the International Baccalaureate (IB) and other qualifications is given in Chapter 3.

What role do dentists have in society?

When researching the profession, most prospective dentists soon realise that it involves much more than gazing into people's mouths all day! It is a challenging vocation that requires a wide range of scientific and personal skills to be mastered in order to be successful.

So why do so many people aspire to study dentistry? Dental professionals often cite a number of positive aspects to pursuing dentistry as a career, which include:

- developing your interest in human anatomy, particularly in relation to the head and mouth
- helping to improve the oral health and confidence of a wide range of people from a range of backgrounds
- being a positive and active member of the local community
- working with your hands, and being able to demonstrate high levels of manual dexterity

- interacting with a wide range of people on a day-to-day basis
- running a business and being your own boss
- flexibility in working hours
- working as part of a team.

Some dentists may also cite the financial benefits and the status and respect that go hand in hand with the career. However, while these factors may play some part in your decision to pursue a career in dentistry, they are certainly not good enough reasons on their own, and would undoubtedly have a negative impact on your application were they ever conveyed to an admissions team.

One of the major focuses of modern dentistry is about general oral health. Dentists are increasingly occupying a much wider societal role than they once had; in addition to carrying out standard treatments, as oral professionals and health practitioners they look after the well-being of their patients and thus become an important part of any community. For example, a dentist may give advice on diet, giving up smoking and its possible knock-on effects for general health, as well as recommendations about courses of dental treatment.

The British Oral Health Foundation has an interesting website, www.dentalhealth.org, which outlines the variety of issues that dentists must consider when treating patients on a daily basis. These include obvious concerns such as dental decay and sensitive teeth, but also more wide-ranging themes such as mouth cancer, diet and bad breath. A quick look through this site should give you an insight into a number of these problems.

In addition to a comprehensive knowledge of the scientific and technical foundation of dentistry, dentists must also have the interpersonal skills required to deal with a wide variety of patients, including those with additional needs. This can pose unique challenges for a dentist; those with physical disabilities may need assistance to get into the dental chair, while people with learning disabilities may become distressed at the thought of going to the dentist and require extra time to be reassured and appropriately cared for. Some patients may have other special needs, such as communication difficulties or being visually or hearing impaired. People with severe medical problems may also need extra care in order to be treated safely and successfully. A dentist must take account of all these and have the skills to deal with them when providing dental care. A dentist may even have to make different arrangements to meet the needs of the individual, and often home visits will need to be organised. Community dental services in the UK currently provide treatment of both old and young people with special medical or social needs, such as complex medical problems, disabilities or mental health problems, who cannot be treated by general dental practitioners (GDPs).

Another major aspect of the role that dentists have in society is education. Along with dental nurses they are at the forefront of teaching the public about good dental hygiene. One of the primary focuses in modern dentistry is on preventive dentistry which aims to promote long-term care of the mouth, teeth, gums and cheeks, and extends, as mentioned earlier, to advice on areas such as diet and lifestyle. Teaching awareness of oral health and hygiene is of paramount importance. Dentists educate patients on caring for their teeth and gums by encouraging them to use a brush with the correct technique, to floss and to use the correct products. Teaching through direct consultations or via literature available in surgeries are just some of the ways that this can be achieved; other ways include the education of young people in schools, and educating elderly people in nursing homes about keeping dentures clean and viable.

Ultimately, the goal of educating the population about oral health and preventive dentistry is to keep the need for major dental treatment to a minimum by maintaining a healthy mouth. The two major causes of tooth loss are tooth decay and gum disease, so the successful prevention of these two problems massively increases the probability of an individual keeping their teeth for life. The joint efforts of the dentist, the hygienist and the patient can help to prevent the need for treatment, and so avoid the pattern of fillings and extractions. This is a saving not only to the individual in terms of time and money but also to the community in the long term.

Dentists can often be the first to spot medical issues that might otherwise go unnoticed until the problem has worsened. One example of this is oral cancer. The most recent published statistics show that there were 12,061 new cases of head and neck cancer in 2015 (this figure accounts for all forms of oral cancer), with 4,047 patients dying from the disease (www.cancerresearchuk.org/health-professional/cancer-statistics/statistics-by-cancer-type/head-and-neck-cancers/incidence#heading-Four). The role of the dentist is therefore vital in early diagnosis and referral for appropriate treatment. Dentists are also the first people to recognise other problems, such as ulcers and cold sores, which could lead to more serious conditions. As with all disease, early recognition is more than half the battle.

Cosmetic dentistry is now a huge industry, with dentists playing a role in providing treatments to straighten, lighten, reshape and repair teeth. Such treatments can include providing veneers, crowns, bridges, tooth-coloured fillings, implants, tooth whitening and correction of bites. Usually abnormal 'bites' or crooked teeth are fixed in childhood, but today even mild abnormalities that have been previously left untreated are seen as a problem and as a consequence more young and mature adults than before are undergoing this type of treatment. The demand for cosmetic treatments continues to grow, due in part to the desire for a flawless smile and, as a result, is a lucrative area for dentists to become involved in.

What are the necessary attributes of a dentist?

As with any highly competitive university course and vocation, in order to succeed candidates must be able to demonstrate their academic ability, the right personal qualities, plus commitment. Practising dentists, admissions tutors and current students all agree that showing genuine dedication to dentistry is essential during the application process, university study and beyond into a dentist's professional life.

It is therefore vital that an applicant to dentistry is certain that they want to be a dentist before applying. Wanting to study dentistry because 'you like science' or because 'you want a job with high employment rates' will not convince an admissions tutor to give you a place. It is also unlikely to be enough to keep you motivated throughout your working life.

Dentistry, unlike medicine, offers fewer diverse pathways or opportunities later on in your career. This ultimately means that you must be fully informed about what the career path entails because it is difficult to move into something else without some degree of re-specialisation.

In addition to being fully committed to dentistry, a dentist must also be able to demonstrate the following:

- the ability to successfully communicate with patients
- an enjoyment in dealing with people and working in a team
- an ability to reassure patients who are scared or in pain
- a caring and sympathetic nature and immense patience
- a high degree of manual dexterity
- self-motivation
- an enjoyment of science
- an interest in current issues in relation to dentistry and oral health
- an excellent memory and an ability to solve problems
- versatility
- mental and physical stamina
- the ability to multi-task between clinical work and the business side of running a practice
- an ability to train and manage people and get the best out of them.

Most of the above qualities should not surprise you. It would be hard to be a successful dentist if you could not bear to be around other people, and unsympathetic dentists end up with few patients. Similarly, if you do not enjoy science, you would be unlikely to gain the necessary grades at A level or pass your exams at university. But often overlooked is the need for stamina when carrying out long and repetitive procedures; concentrating on one thing for hours might not be for you if you struggle to maintain concentration!

If you believe that you have at least some of the qualities listed above, the next step is to investigate what being a dentist is actually like and to find out what a dentist does. In brief, a dentist's job can include a range of tasks, for example carrying out routine examinations, filling cavities, examining X-rays, applying protective sealant on teeth, extracting teeth, removing decay, fitting dental implants, taking measurements and making models for dentures. This gives a small glimpse into the versatility needed by a practising dentist.

Many people are unaware that dentists are usually self-employed, and the amount of money they earn is directly related to the number of patients they see. Without stamina and self-motivation, as well as some degree of business acumen, you are unlikely to earn as much as you might hope.

Research by the Institute for Fiscal Studies (IFS) released in 2017 (last published date) revealed that the average student debt was £50,000 (https://www.ifs.org.uk/publications/9334). While studying at university, many students accrue multiple debts, including student loans (tuition fee and maintenance loans), overdrafts, credit cards, debts to parents and sometimes even commercial loans. Therefore, once qualified, dentists need to earn enough not only to support themselves but also to begin paying off these debts. It should also be remembered that the average student debt figure of £50,000 is largely based on three-year degree courses, so the average figure for a dental student is likely to be even higher.

As part of the government's Teaching Excellence Framework (TEF), which ranks English universities and colleges based on the quality of their teaching, universities that have a TEF award can charge up to the maximum amount (£9,250). Universities without a TEF award can only charge up to £9,000 per year. It is likely that student fees will continue to rise in line with inflation in coming years, so levels of student debt are expected to continue to rise.

Are there any downsides to being a dentist?

There are, of course, some negative aspects of dentistry. Some of the common downsides that dentists cite relate to issues including stress, the demanding nature of being self-employed, lack of career progression, aggressive or frightened patients, and, last but by no means least, the boredom that can accompany repetitive routine tasks. If you are worried about any of these, you should talk to your own dentist to see how he or she feels about them.

Before looking at the applications and admissions processes in more detail, you may be interested to read what a current dental student had to say about her choice of career thus far. Bear in mind that this could be you in one or two years' time.

Case study: Yusra Khan, first-year dentistry student

'My interest in pursuing a career in dentistry began while visiting family abroad. I observed the lack of dental hygiene and an absence in preventative measures especially in school-aged children, which contrasted with dentistry in the UK. I noticed that there were many disparities within local areas, and often dental care was not up to par. This led me to want to educate parents and children in my area. I started distributing information leaflets about brushing techniques and how to prevent caries. When I returned home, I decided that I wanted to carry on pursuing the same goals of improving oral health in the UK.

'Prior to applying, I undertook work experience for three weeks in a dental practice and for one week in an orthodontic and maxillo-facial clinic at a hospital. I was also able to witness an extraction under general anaesthetic. From this work experience, I learnt a variety of transferrble skills from both the dentist and the dental nurse. I was particularly impressed by the techniques used when managing an anxious patient and the steps that must be put in place when a patient has additional needs.

'My journey to securing my place to study dentistry was a tough one, but through perseverance and dedication I was able to secure the grades I needed to study at the University of Leeds. Since starting the course, I have particularly enjoyed learning something new each day and that I have been able to build step-by-step on the foundation I laid during A levels.

'My tips for prospective students are:
- be prepared for long days at university and a heavy workload
- much of the work in some modules is self-taught, so be ready to go out and research tasks independently – you won't get everything spoon-fed to you
- find a great group of friends who have a similar mindset to you and enjoy your time in university!'

1 | Studying dentistry

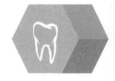

According to UCAS, in 2017 there were 9,240 applicants for entry into dentistry courses competing for 1,135 places, a ratio of 8.14 applicants per place. The ratio of female to male applicants was about 61:39, with 720 women gaining places – significantly higher than the 415 men accepted. Male applicants had a slightly lower success rate of 12%, compared to 13% for female applicants. It is clear from scrutinising the application statistics over the last eight years that there are some significant patterns in dentistry applications related to gender; there have consistently been more applications and more places gained by females in comparison with their male counterparts (see Table 1 opposite). There are undoubtedly numerous reasons behind this, but it is certain that this is a sustained pattern that is not just due to chance.

Around 365 of the total number of applicants were from the EU (excluding the UK), with only 15 being accepted, which represents a success rate of just over 4%. For other non-EU international students, there were 1,050 applicants, with only 75 being accepted, a success rate of approximately 7%. This demonstrates that it is far more difficult for your application to be successful if you are an overseas applicant, and the reasons for this are discussed further in Chapter 7.

In recent years, it has become obvious that total applicant numbers for dentistry have been steadily declining; since 2010, there has been a 29% decrease in applications (see Table 1). However, there was a small increase of 2% in overall applications between 2016 and 2017. One of the most noticeable statistics in relation to the fall in applicants is that it has been largely driven by fewer men applying; since 2010, male applications have fallen 38%, while female applications have decreased by 22%.

There are likely to be a number of factors that have caused this dip in numbers, with the most important one likely being the introduction of £9,000 tuition fees in 2012. However, despite this decrease in numbers, it is clear that there is still an extremely strong demand for places on dental courses and the success rates are still relatively low. Prospective dental students should therefore ensure that they are not lulled into a false sense of security; a dip in applications does not mean significantly easier entry! As has always been the case, top grades and thorough preparation are irreplaceable when trying to make a successful application.

Table 1 UCAS End of Cycle Applicant statistics for dentistry – 2010–17

Year	Applicants	Places	Applicants per place	Male applications	Males gaining places	Female applications	Females gaining places	Male success rate	Female success rate	Overseas applications (EU/Non-EU)
2017	9240	1135	8.14	3565	415	5675	720	12%	13%	365/1050
2016	9060	1100	8.24	3575	430	5485	670	12%	12%	465/1160
2015	9875	1095	9.02	3920	410	5960	685	10%	11%	490/1320
2014	11210	1100	10.14	4360	395	6850	705	9%	10%	515/1225
2013	11350	1185	9.54	4725	460	6625	725	10%	11%	635/1100
2012	11630	1195	9.73	5010	470	6615	725	9%	11%	600/1185
2011	12550	1195	10.50	5670	510	6880	685	9%	10%	775/1170
2010	13055	1280	10.20	5790	525	7268	755	9%	10%	905/1020
% change 2016–17	+2%	+3%	0%	0%	−3%	+3%	+7%			
% change 2010–17	−29%	−11%	−20%	−38%	−21%	−22%	−5%			

Source: www.ucas.com/data-and-analysis/ucas-undergraduate-releases/ucas-undergraduate-end-cycle-data-resources.
We acknowledge UCAS' contribution of this information.

Exploring the options

So what are the steps that you need to take to ensure that you have an excellent chance of being selected for an interview and offered a place?

The first step is to thoroughly research the stages of the application process and the demands of the course and career. This is vital for a number of reasons. You need to:

- see whether dentistry is the right career for you
- see whether your personal and academic skills are matched to the course
- find out which universities offer dentistry and to which you want to apply
- find out the details of courses offered by each university and the one that might best suit you (while the courses may have the same title, their structures can differ)
- find out the academic requirements for the course and which pre-admissions test is needed
- gain ideas and information about possible work experience placements
- find out what makes an excellent personal statement
- understand the demands of the interview process and to develop interview skills.

Ideally, your research should start in the first year of your A levels (Fifth year in Scotland) or even earlier; the most committed prospective dentists I meet often start their preparation in year 10 or before. Most schools start a programme of UCAS and career prospects-related workshops halfway through the first year of A levels, with the aim being that students should have a clear idea about where they want to apply after the summer holidays. However, you should make your mind up about studying dentistry as soon as possible to give you the maximum amount of time for research and work experience placements.

There are several sources that can be used for research. These can be divided into:

- media research: internet, books, prospectuses and specialist magazines
- discussion with professionals
- work experience.

Some suggestions for media research are given below.

Internet

There are a wide variety of resources available on the internet that are useful for researching the profession and for preparing for interviews.

- The UCAS website (www.ucas.com) is initially the most useful for research into degree courses and gives comprehensive details about the entry requirements and course structure at each university.
- Newspaper sites: the *Guardian* (www.guardian.com/education/universityguide) and the *Times* (www.thetimes.co.uk) provide useful information about university league tables and subject rankings. Please note that the *Times* can only be accessed via a subscription.
- The British Dental Association (www.bda.org) gives information primarily on topical issues for healthcare professionals.
- The Oral Health Foundation (www.dentalhealth.org) focuses more on raising public awareness of important oral hygiene issues. This website is useful if you want to gain a wider understanding of public health issues in relation to dentistry.
- www.dentistry.co.uk and www.the-dentist.co.uk are very useful online periodicals offering up-to-date information.
- News websites: sites like the BBC news website (www.bbc.co.uk/news) have up-to-date articles about current affairs related to dentistry and health.
- University websites: most of the information you will need about applying to a university and about the course can be found on individual universities' websites. These are a treasure trove of information and will help you get a feel for each institution and the nature of the course it is offering.
- The Complete University Guide (www.thecompleteuniversityguide.co.uk) and Unistats (https://unistats.direct.gov.uk) websites provide impartial information relating to universities and courses. These are useful resources to help find out information relating to student feedback, satisfaction scores and employment rates.

Books, magazines and prospectuses

- *HEAP 2020: University Degree Course Offers* by Brian Heap has a short section on dentistry and the universities offering dentistry courses, and gives a good overview of entry requirements.
- University prospectuses: visiting each university website and requesting a prospectus will help you get a feel for the institution and the course. Note that a number of universities have full prospectuses online.
- Subscribing to magazines such as *The Dentist* will let you find out first-hand about issues and developments in dentistry. This would be seen as extracurricular reading and would demonstrate your interest to university admissions panels.

Case study: Simran Chahal

'I chose to study dentistry because it was a career that I was really passionate about following my work experience. During my GCSEs, I was totally adamant that I wanted to be a lawyer and hence chose to do my work experience placement in a law firm. It was a life lesson for sure! I didn't enjoy it one bit and went back to the drawing board, I looked at what I enjoyed at school and where my strengths were. I looked into dentistry following the recommendations of some of my friends that had already applied to university and decided to carry out some work experience within the field.

'It wasn't just the skills required for the profession that drew me in but the fact that you are able to meet so many people each day, each with their own stories and backgrounds. Furthermore, dentistry is a career that doesn't ever end, throughout your life you will always be learning as the industry develops, and this is something that really excites me! My job will never get boring! When you begin to study dentistry you will soon come to realise that there are numerous area of specialisation and options for branching out into different fields.

'Working in clinics in deprived areas of the country has brought to light the impact that "simple" procedures, such as scaling and polishing, can have on patients, and how improved oral health can potentially change an individual's life.

'Before applying, I carried out a bulk of my work experience during my first year of A levels over a prolonged period at a local practice. Additionally, I was able to shadow in the oral maxillofacial department at a hospital in Birmingham.

'My placement in the dental surgery showed me how important teamwork is; if there isn't a nurse present a lot of disruption is caused. It has become even more apparent since starting my own training. I also saw how empathy and being non-judgemental were of vital importance; there could be a number of factors that contribute to the state of a person's oral hygiene and so it is important not to jump to conclusions.

'Since starting my course, I have had to work really hard, but have also had lots of rewarding experiences. A lot of people on my course found the jump between A levels and undergraduate study tough. You have to become independent, motivate yourself to do the best and stay on top of your study. At the end of my first year I treated several patients and carried out a large number of clinical procedures on the phantom heads. These next few years excite me as I will slowly become more capable of carrying out clinical procedures and be able to treat an increasing number of people!

'The clinical aspect of the course is by far the most enjoyable and makes the 8 a.m. starts worthwhile. As a student you are able to spend a lot longer with patients, meaning that you are able to get to know them as a person and build a relationship with them. The hardest part is when it comes to summer or a referral and you have to discharge them!

In terms of challenges, I find it difficult to make time for my friends outside of the course, because they have a lot more free time and you can't always afford to socialise with them until late in the evening or you're just too tired to even go out! However, it does get easier as you adjust to a new routine and find a balance.

'My tips for aspiring dentists are:
- ensure you stay on top of study from the start, it will help you so much when it comes to exams
- try and improve your manual dexterity skills before you start university
- if you're looking to apply to university, have a look at when they start clinics and actually treat patients; some universities start later than others and you could wait three years to realise that you don't like the job at all
- don't be put off by the interview process
- be prepared for long hours
- get plenty of experience in as many aspects as you can.'

University courses

In the UK, the General Dental Council (GDC) publishes a document that outlines the requirements of all dental programmes leading to GDC registration. These 'Standards for Education' (www.gdc-uk.org/professionals/education) ensure that all dental schools have to deal with a prescribed set of learning outcomes over the duration of the course. This means that there is a significant degree of similarity between the dental courses offered at different universities. However, it is also vital to remember that different dental schools will have different ways of approaching these outcomes, and consequently course structure and teaching approaches may differ greatly; this can ultimately result in massively different experiences for students when studying dentistry. It is therefore vital that you thoroughly research how each course is structured so that they can truly understand what it will be like to study dentistry at a particular university. This section therefore aims to give you some idea of the key things you will experience as a dental student throughout the duration of your studies.

Undergraduate

Studying dentistry in the UK is a challenging but highly rewarding experience, and the provision at British dental schools is normally first rate. Prospective students should be aware from the outset that undertaking this course will require commitment and dedication; ask any current dental student and they will tell you how much hard work is needed to succeed. Undergraduate dental courses last for five years and at the end of their studies students will gain the initials BDS or BChD (the Latin equivalent of BDS) after their name. There is no distinction between these two classifications as both refer to a Bachelor of Dental Surgery; the distinction depends on the dental school that a student has attended.

As outlined above, most of the dental schools have a similar structure in their courses but key differences have begun to emerge in the teaching methodology and delivery of course content. It is therefore important for students to carefully research the details of each course and appreciate the key features. This is obviously vital in selecting an appropriate dental school, submitting a relevant personal statement and preparing for an interview. Many of the dental schools have started to put a greater emphasis on students taking responsibility for their own learning. At Leeds, for example, much emphasis is placed on clinical dentistry throughout the course, with first clinical exposure occurring in year 1.

Integrated learning, problem-based learning (PBL) and enquiry-based learning (EBL)

Universities teach in a range of ways, from traditional large lectures to small tuition groups; however, most faculties employ a wide range of methods to ensure their students develop into highly competent practitioners. Some schools, such as Liverpool, have successfully developed courses that have some elements of problem-based learning (PBL) at their core. Many of the dental schools have begun to place a greater responsibility on students to be accountable for their own learning, and prospective students should be aware of terms such as enquiry-based learning (EBL), self-directed learning and computer-based learning.

These approaches are designed to develop an independent and inquisitive approach to learning, using libraries and discussing issues with colleagues to solve problems (as the name suggests). Bristol, by contrast, does not explicitly use the PBL approach, and adopts a system based on lectures, workshops, tutorials and practical sessions. Many courses integrate elements of clinical contact from the first year of the course, while others do not introduce clinical contact until year two. At Birmingham and Cardiff, for example, first-year students will have exposure to clinical contact for one day per week, whereas at Bristol and Plymouth, clinical teaching and patient treatment begin in the second year. As you would expect, all dental schools are committed to using up-to-date technology to help teach the curriculum, and students will notice how keen the various dental schools are to demonstrate this during open days. A basic summary of teaching styles employed in each of the dental schools is summarised below.

Table 2 Teaching styles

Dental school	Teaching style(s)
University of Aberdeen (graduates only)	Integrated
University of Birmingham	Integrated/EBL
University of Bristol	Integrated
Cardiff University	Integrated
University of Central Lancashire (graduates only)	Integrated
University of Dundee	Integrated
University of Glasgow	Integrated
King's College London	Integrated
University of Leeds	Integrated
University of Liverpool	Integrated/PBL
University of Manchester	Integrated/EBL
Newcastle University	Integrated
University of Plymouth	Integrated
Queen Mary, University of London	Integrated
Queen's University Belfast	Integrated
University of Sheffield	Integrated

Course structure

Year one

The reason why a dental course lasts five years is that the teaching covers a wide variety of elements. All dental schools will offer one or two years of pre-clinical study that lays the biological foundation for the rest of the course and clinical practice. This is often taught outside the school and covers numerous themes such as:

- anatomy
- oral health and disease
- biochemistry
- physiology
- biochemistry
- microbiology
- oral biology
- cell biology.

In addition, students will often cover introductory modules related to communication, interpersonal skills, clinical competence and team-working skills, due to the patient-centred nature of the profession. Many dental schools will also introduce some limited clinical exposure in the first year.

Years two to five

As the course progresses, the amount of clinical work that you carry out will increase, with most universities offering increased levels of clinical contact from the second year. Alongside your clinical and skill develop-ment work, you will continue with programmes in areas such as oral biology, disease and pathology. You will also learn about the social and psychological aspects of patient care while developing your interper-sonal and communication skills.

As the clinical part of the course increases in importance, students will usually take responsibility for their own patients. During the third year of the programme at Birmingham, for example, students are given respon-sibility for their own patients' treatment in what amounts to their own mini-practice in the dental hospital. Students will also spend time in other settings, such as dental access centres, general dental practices or community practices to gain practical experience. Some courses involve spending time in local hospitals to gain experience of the sec-ondary care that takes place following a referral from a dentist. In order to teach the patient care necessary to treat a range of people effec-tively, there may be modules in behavioural sciences and the manage-ment of pain and anxiety, as well as in the treatment of children, the elderly and disabled people. Clinical students will typically study some of the following courses (full details of each course can be found on individual university websites):

- dental materials science
- dental public health
- haematology
- operative technique and clinical skills
- paediatric dentistry
- restorative dentistry
- oral medicine and surgery
- oral pathology
- oral biochemistry and biology
- oral diseases
- orthodontics
- endodontics
- prosthodontics
- periodontics
- pharmacology
- nutrition and diet
- medico-legal and ethical aspects of dental practice

- forensic dentistry
- sedation
- behavioural science
- oral radiography
- communication skills
- management and leadership
- social and behavioural science.

Some universities offer their students the opportunity to complete an intercalated BSc. This is normally a one-year project, during which time you pause your dentistry degree and investigate a chosen topic in much more depth. This usually results in securing an additional degree before rejoining the course the following year.

Your final years of study consist primarily of further development of clinical skills to consolidate the knowledge and skills that you have previously acquired and prepare you for practising once you have qualified. You will continue to have extensive and varied clinical exposure in a number of settings outside of the dental school throughout this time. There is also further academic work that continues alongside the practical components. As you near the end of your clinical course, you may have time to pursue your own elective programme of study – a topic of personal interest, which you research on your own.

At the end of year five, there is the final BDS/BChD professional examination. On successful completion of the course, graduates are competent to carry out most treatments and exercise independent clinical judgement.

Two examples of course outlines are provided in the boxes below to illustrate the common threads and differences between different universities.

Programme structure: University of Plymouth (2019)

You will treat patients through partnership with Peninsula Dental Social Enterprise and the wider NHS in Devon and Cornwall, become familiar with a variety of clinical situations, and prepare for a future career path through solving clinical problems. You'll also discover how clinical dentistry and research is practiced in different social and cultural contexts in other parts of the South-west, the rest of the UK and across the world.

Year 1

Your clinical education commences at the start of Year 1, working in small, integrated study groups you will learn the core scientific foundations of dentistry in a clinical context, explore the scientific basis of normal structure, function and behaviour, with a focus on dental health, prevention of dental disease and the underlying principles of personal and professional development. You will attend the Simulated Dental Learning Environment (SDLE) from your first week developing essential clinical skills and in Term 2 you will experience contact with patients in the clinics where you will be able to develop your communication skills under the close supervision of dental practitioners, bringing to life the skills gained in SDLE. Near the end of the year you have your first experience in social engagement.

Core modules

- DEN411 Integrated Dental Science 1
- DEN412 Clinical Dental Practice 1
- DEN413 Clinical Dental Practice 2
- DEN414 Inter-Professional Engagement 1
- DEN415 Professional Development 1

Year 2

In your second year, you build on your foundations with common dental problems, as well as disease mechanisms considered in much greater depth. Learning continues in SDLE as you develop skills for advanced procedures while continuing to care for patients in the clinics in Plymouth two days per week. You gain insight into the importance of team working in dentistry as you integrate with other members of the team in the clinical environment, and plan and deliver a social engagement project intervention.

Core modules

- DEN521 Integrated Dental Science 2
- DEN522 Clinical Dental Practice 3
- DEN523 Clinical Dental Practice 4
- DEN524 Inter-Professional Engagement 2
- DEN525 Professional Development 2

Year 3

In your Year 3 there is greater self-directed learning as you prepare project assignments, including an engagement project with students from another healthcare profession, and clinical cases. Based in Plymouth with transport provided to our Exeter clinic two days per week you build upon existing skills and consolidate advanced procedures provided for patients. One of the themes for years three and four is to consolidate the learning of medically-related issues for the safe practise of dentistry. You will be given an opportunity to learn about dentally relevant medical issues in patient-based demonstrations.

Core modules

- DEN631 Applied Dental Knowledge 1
- DEN632 Critical Appraisal 1
- DEN633 Clinical Dental Practice 5
- DEN634 Clinical Dental Practice 6
- DEN635 Inter-Professional Engagement 3
- DEN636 Professional Development 3

Intercalated Master of Science (MSc)

Selected students may intercalate, between Year 3 and Year 4, and undertake a one year MSc in our research laboratories in Plymouth.

Year 4

In your fourth year you will live in Truro for the whole academic year. Clinical activity will expand to three days per week and you start to prepare clinical cases for Finals. Clinical dentistry will now embrace all of the aspects of dental care provision expected of a qualified dentist, will give you experience in advanced restorative techniques and strengthen your competence in treatment planning. You'll gain first-hand experience of the role and services provided by specialists in primary and secondary care, by spending time in specialist clinics such as restorative dentistry, oral surgery, oral diseases and orthodontics.

Core modules

- DEN641 Applied Dental Knowledge 2
- DEN642 Clinical Dental Practice 7
- DEN643 Inter-Professional Engagement 4
- DEN644 Professional Development 4

Final year

The emphasis in your final year is on the implementation and consolidation of the skills and abilities you have learned in previous years and is the final preparation for dental practice. You will become more confident with clinical situations, healthcare teams and the principles of professionalism; and discover advances in dentistry being developed for future practice.

Core modules

- DEN651 Applied Dental Knowledge 3
- DEN652 Clinical Dental Practice 8
- DEN653 Clinical Dental Practice 9
- DEN654 Inter-Professional Engagement 5
- DEN655 Professional Development 5

Source: www.plymouth.ac.uk/courses/undergraduate/
bds-dental-surgery.
Reprinted with kind permission of the University of Plymouth.

Programme structure: University of Manchester (2019)

The Bachelor of Dental Surgery (BDS) course will prepare you for a dentistry career through a combination of clinical study and basic and advanced dental sciences. Once you have mastered basic competencies in the skills facilities, you will move on to treating patients in both the Dental Hospital and local outreach clinics early in the course. You will learn to work within a dental team to take a patient-centred approach to clinical care, practicing in a professional, safe and ethical manner. Students are also trained to become reflective practitioners who are committed to lifelong learning.

Special features

Early clinical experience
You will be introduced to the clinical environment in the first semester of Year 1, enabling you to integrate theory and practice early on in the course.

Interdisciplinary learning
Learn alongside students and professionals from a range of backgrounds, including those training in complementary professions such as dental nursing and therapy.

Intercalation opportunities
You can study another subject to achieve a BSc award over one year between Years 2 and 3 of the BDS course.

Foundation year available
Students who do not have the required science qualifications for Year 1 entry but have achieved good grades in other non-science subjects may apply for the BDS with Foundation Year .

Course content for year 1

Basic building blocks:

- Orofacial Biology 1
- Healthy Living 1 (a healthy body)
- Team Working, Professionalism and Patient Management 1
- Patient Assessment 1

Course content for year 2

Building your knowledge, skills and attitudes:

- Orofacial Biology 2
- Healthy Living 2 (a healthy mouth)
- Team Working, Professionalism and Patient Management 2
- Patient Assessment 2
- Disease Management 2

Course content for year 3

Integrating knowledge, skills and attitudes:

- Orofacial Biology 3
- Healthy Living 3 (a healthy mind)
- Team Working, Professionalism and Patient Management 3
- Patient Assessment 3
- Disease Management 3
- Participation in the Manchester Leadership Programme (MLP)

Course content for year 4

Achieving clinical competence:

- Orofacial Biology 4
- Team Working, Professionalism and Patient Management 4
- Patient Assessment 4
- Disease Management 4

Course content for year 5

Moving to professional competence:

- Team Working, Professionalism and Patient Management 5
- Preparation for Independent Practice
- The Complex Patient

Source: www.bmh.manchester.ac.uk/study/undergraduate/courses/2019/
bds-dentistry-first-year-entry/?pg=2#course-profile.
Reprinted with kind permission from the University of Manchester.

Postgraduate

There are many opportunities for postgraduate study in a variety of dental subjects. It is worth noting, however, that before any form of clinical training can commence (i.e. training involving hands-on contact with patients), dental graduates must register with the GDC. Dental schools and hospitals run a wide range of postgraduate programmes that include further clinical and non-clinical training and research degree programmes. The postgraduate courses may be offered as a diploma, master's degree or doctorate and may take from one to two years, or in a few cases can be flexibly completed over a period of up to five years. Many courses are offered on a part-time basis and can therefore comfortably fit around full-time employment.

General advice and guidance is available from the Royal College of Surgeons of England (RCS) website (www.rcseng.ac.uk/dental-faculties/fds). Within this site are links to each of the universities offering postgraduate courses (www.rcseng.ac.uk/dental-faculties/fds/nacpde/postgraduate-dental-courses). If you can't find the information you need here, visit the website of the individual university directly for the most detailed, up-to-date information.

At Newcastle University, for example, there are four taught programmes. These are:

- Clinical Implant Dentistry PGDip
- Conscious Sedation PGDip
- Orthodontics MSc
- Restorative Dentistry MClinDent

Programme details: Orthodontics at Newcastle University (2019)

The course is designed to equip you with the knowledge and skills required to complement your clinical training and aims to provide:

- knowledge to support the clinical treatment of orthodontic cases, including simple and complex cases appropriate for specialist practitioner level
- an evidence base for orthodontics and the skills required to appraise the evidence base
- applied research within orthodontics.

The course provides theoretical teaching to support the development of an orthodontic specialist. We provide a comprehensive seminar programme incorporating the theoretical and diagnostic elements of specialist knowledge, and the opportunity to carry out a research project allied to our research strategy. Our course includes:

- normal and abnormal development of the dentition
- tooth movements and facial orthopaedics
- orthodontic materials
- orthodontic biomechanics
- orthodontic techniques
- biological sciences relevant to orthodontics
- an overview of multidisciplinary orthodontics.

The aim of the research component is to expose you to the principles and practicalities of performing dental research. Projects range from laboratory studies, analysis of new data sets, systematic reviews and short-term clinical studies.

Research projects are identified and allocated during the first term. By the end of the first year you will have completed your first draft of your literature review and have established your methodology. More time is available for research during the second and third years with the dissertation handed in at the end of January of the third year. You will be encouraged to publish your research work in scientific journals.

The course has been running for two decades and has a good national reputation. Graduates have gone on to work in prestigious practices, senior academic posts and in hospital consultant positions.

Source: www.ncl.ac.uk/postgraduate/courses/degrees/orthodontics-msc/#profile.
Reprinted with kind permission of Newcastle University.

Other universities are also able to provide a wide range of postgraduate options. At King's College London, for example, there are 10 taught graduate programmes, six of which can be pursued via distance learning.

While undertaking a postgraduate qualification is not mandatory, it is an excellent way to specialise in a particular area of interest. This can ultimately result in enhanced career prospects and earning potential in the long run.

In addition to the more formal postgraduate qualifications, qualified dentists are also required to participate in a specified amount of mandatory continuous professional development (CPD). This comprises short courses for qualified dentists who want to develop their knowledge of the latest methods, equipment and techniques. It is the GDC that specifies the requirements for CPD for dental professionals, and CPD is offered by numerous institutions around the country.

2 | Getting work experience

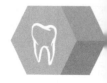

Discussing your interest in dentistry with dentists working in the field is an excellent way of gathering first-hand information about the subject. It may be a good idea to start by talking to your own local dentist or any family members or friends who are dentists. Discuss with them their experiences of studying dentistry and about the career options and prospects for dentists. Remember to ask about the negative points about the profession as well as the positives, as practising dentists are the individuals who are best placed to answer these questions openly and honestly. It would also be worth asking about what they perceive to be the most relevant and interesting current issues in the world of dentistry as they are going to have the most up-to-date insight.

Following on from these initial discussions, it is then essential to organise, either by yourself or via your school, some work experience where you will be able to work-shadow a dentist and see a practice in action. Shadowing dentists is useful as it will help you to get an insight into the demands of the profession and decide whether you really want to be a dentist. You will find out what goes on in a dental surgery and some of the responsibilities that a dentist has to fulfil, as well as giving you an opportunity to ask questions. It will also demonstrate your commitment to admissions tutors.

It is vital to remember that undertaking relevant work placements prior to applying is now a prerequisite; it is unlikely that you will be considered unless you have evidence of two weeks' worth of experience. Even more importantly, work experience is a chance for you to decide whether dentistry is the right career for you. I have seen numerous students who have expressed a desire to be a dentist but then totally changed their minds after a week of shadowing and observation. Conversely, I have also seen many students who have shown increased dedication to pursuing a career in dentistry following work experience.

Due to the continued competitiveness of the application process, in addition to a mininum of two weeks' work experience, it is advisable to try to demonstrate an ongoing commitment to the field of dentistry. This means that you should ideally aim to spend time with several different dentists on a regular basis over a number of months. While the basic two weeks can often be enough, anything extra will serve to strengthen your application. Preparation for your application to study dentistry must therefore start as soon as possible, preferably in the first year of your A levels (Fifth year in Scotland) or earlier; if you decide on dentistry as a career only at the start of your second A level year (Sixth year in Scotland), it will leave little or no time to build up a solid portfolio of work experience.

How to arrange work experience

Some schools and colleges have schemes whereby they can organise work experience for you. However, where these schemes exist, it is unlikely that they will provide every placement for you, and so at some point you will have to show initiative by making the necessary arrangements. There are two routes that you should try: approaching local dentists, and making use of contacts that your friends or family may have.

In order to approach local dentists about possible work experience, you should first get the names and addresses of local dental practices from a website such as the Yellow Pages (www.yell.co.uk) or the BDA (www.bda.org). You should then write a formal email or letter, and include the name of a referee (that is, someone who can vouch for your interest in dentistry as well as your reliability). Your careers teacher, housemaster/housemistress or form teacher would be ideal as a referee. An example of a suitable email is given in the box below.

Dear Mr Littlewood [phone the practice first to find the name of the dentist you should address the email to]

I am currently in my first year of studying A levels in Biology, Chemistry, Maths and Psychology at Shuttlefield School, and I am interested in pursuing a career in dentistry. I was wondering if it would be possible to meet you to discuss what the profession is like and then perhaps spend a week shadowing you or one of your colleagues, so that I can get some first-hand experience.

If you require a reference, please contact my form tutor, Mr Jones. His contact details are as follows:

Mr T. Jones
Shuttlefield School
Shuttlefield
SH21 2CF

I look forward to hearing from you.

Yours sincerely

Mr Robert Smith

Things to look out for during work experience

Your work experience will provide you with invaluable opportunities to develop your knowledge and understanding of dentistry as a career. It is therefore vital that you pay close attention to what is going on around you so you can get the most from the experience.

Make sure you are as professional as possible throughout your placements: dress formally and be on your best behaviour at all times. Turn your phone off and put it away so that it's not a distraction. Ask intelligent questions to further your understanding of what is going on. Offer to help the dentist or the receptionists with routine tasks. Show an interest in all that is going on around you, bearing in mind that this might be your job in a few years' time. It is also vital to buy a notebook and keep it handy during your placements. You should keep a record of:

- any procedures you observe
- any interesting, shocking or unusual cases you observe
- any reflections on your time spent shadowing.

During your placements, you should pay attention to the following aspects of dental practice.

The attributes of a dentist

Dentists need to be much more than dental treatment robots; it is therefore a good idea to keep a note of the range of characteristics the dentist demonstrates on a day-to-day basis as well as the variety of tasks they carry out. This will help provide you with a list of the sort of skills you will need to develop as a dentist and will ultimately help you in developing the knowledge of dentists you will require to write a personal statement and have a successful interview.

Interactions with patients

A vital part of the dentist's role is to interact with patients to discuss potential treatment routes and to guide and reassure them. Take time to observe how a dentist communicates with patients, particularly those who are anxious about being treated or have special needs.

The variety of treatments available to patients

Make sure that you know what you are observing during your placement. Ask the dentist or nurse for the technical names of the procedures you see and for information on the materials and equipment used. Ask about the advantages and disadvantages of different types of filling, implant or denture.

Make sure that you are aware not only of the way that damaged teeth are repaired, but also about preventive dentistry, orthodontics and oral hygiene. You should also try to discuss the dentist's role in identifying other problems, such as oral cancer.

The roles of different team members

In any dental setting, there will be a wide range of individuals involved who are vital to the overall functioning of the team. For example, in addition to the dentist there may also be dental nurses, hygienists, receptionists and administrators. Make sure you take time to talk to as many members of the team as possible and ask them about the role they play.

Working as a dentist

Ask the dentist about his or her professional life. Find out about the hours, the way in which dentists are paid, the demands of the job and the career options. Find out what dentists like about the job and what they dislike.

Ultimately, being observant and asking questions will help you further your understanding of what is required in being a dentist. At the end of each of your placements, you should ask yourself whether this is still a career path that you wish to pursue. If there are any aspects of the work that you dislike, ask yourself whether these would put you off becoming a dentist.

The importance of voluntary work

In addition to undertaking work experience directly related to dentistry, it is also essential to show evidence or experience of any voluntary work that you have undertaken. The most useful voluntary work to undertake would be in a care-based environment, for example, a hospital, a children's hospice or a nursing home. Second best would be voluntary work in settings such as schools, youth clubs and community groups. Still useful, but least desirable would be time spent in a charity shop. Most charitable organisations are always eager to recruit volunteers to help out, so these kinds of experience are usually far easier to arrange than a placement in a dental surgery.

The point of carrying out voluntary work is to demonstrate the caring side of your personality and also develop your ability to deal with people. If you have been able to put together a well-developed portfolio of experience, it will go a long way to demonstrate to admissions tutors that you are really devoted to working with and helping people. It will also help to develop your understanding of the wider world and other clinical environments and so ultimately strengthen your application.

Case study: Anika Kanda, second-year dentistry student

'One of the main reasons that I decided to pursue a career in dentistry was because I want to be able to help people in a health-care capacity and go into something that relies on interacting and communicating with people, which is something that I enjoy. For me, dentistry is the perfect combination of science and the arts, which I believe are my two strengths and so nothing seemed more appealing to me than this hands-on, intellectually stimulating career!

'Prior to applying, I tried to get a range of different work experiences in the dental field to be able to get an idea of the different specialties that dentistry offers. I carried out placements at two different NHS General Dental Practices as well as a private practice to see the similarities and differences between them. I also shadowed some dentists who had specialised, such as an orthodontist and a dentist who worked in Special Care dentistry with people with disabilities or those who are very nervous. To further explore the different aspects of the dental profession, I also worked with a team of technicians at a denture factory. Here I obtained some enjoyable practical experience by attempting some dental construction myself, such as casting impressions and wax modelling.

'What I gained most out of my work experiences was witnessing the rapport between the dentists and the patients, and how important it is to build a relationship in order to give their professional judgement and to reassure them if they are nervous. I also saw the importance of working in a team, and not only with your dental nurse whom you have a "four-handed relationship" with, but also with the other professionals, such as the hygienists and therapists. Doing work experience at the denture factory illustrated to me the importance of communication between dentists and other agencies, such as the dental technician which all work to a tight timescale to provide an exceptional service. Often the materials made had to go back and forth between the clinic and the lab if they didn't fit, so good communication was required.

'I really enjoy the clinical aspect of the course where we get the chance to go to the dental hospital and observe patients being treated by the older dental students, as this gives a sense of what is to come following on from first year. I also enjoy learning more about the role of a dentist and the importance of communication skills, as well as discussing ethical dilemmas in dentistry, as these are normally quite difficult and require some thought.

'Studying dentistry is very demanding and full on, and often it is sometimes hard to balance work life with socialising at university as the course involves long days which many other courses may not have. Therefore, it is important for me to always bear in mind my end goal to keep me motivated and enthusiastic when the work load is getting too much. I also found that in the first year you are taught a lot of things that feel as though they may not be relevant to dentistry, for example doing biochemistry practicals and learning about parts of the body we wouldn't think we would need to. However, we were assured by our lecturers that it is all an integral part of our understanding and everything does come together eventually.

'My tips for prospective students are:

- be organised and be on top of your work load, and don't underestimate how much time and effort is required of you; this was especially difficult for me when needing to balance preparing for my interviews and studying for my A levels
- be passionate about dentistry and let this come across in your personal statement and interviews – research, read about it and be knowledgeable about it
- enjoy the whole process – even though it can be stressful at times, it is still a chance to learn more about yourself and develop your understanding for the career you hope to have in the future.'

Making the most of your work experience and voluntary work

The notebook that you record the details of your experiences in will quickly become a personal diary of what you have completed, and this will be an invaluable resource when it comes to writing a personal statement. Should you be offered an interview, it is extremely likely that you will be asked questions about the experiences you have shared in your statement, so including details you have recorded will give you a chance to talk about a topic you are at ease with.

Start by noting down the dates and duration of each of your placements; this is a vital element that will need to be included in your personal statement to show that you have not just done the minimum amount of experience to be considered. Often, I meet students that have done months and months of work experience, but have undersold themselves by not giving this level of detail.

Following this, make sure you note down descriptions of what you have done or seen each day; try to remember names of specific treatments or procedures that you have seen and remember to ask if you don't know the technical name of a procedure or a piece of equipment. This will allow you to build an understanding of some of the technical terminology used in the profession and help you to build an understanding of the day-to-day responsibilities of a dentist.

Finally, the most important thing for you to do is to carry out deep reflection on the time you have spent undertaking work experience and voluntary placements. It is vital that you go beyond simple descriptions of what you have seen and delve more into what stood out to you and what your thoughts and feelings were, as this will demonstrate that you really engaged with what you saw.

Case study: Ayesha Mohamed, second-year dentistry student

'A career in dentistry was extremely appealing to me since it combined patient interaction, my desire to work closely with people and the ability to use my scientific knowledge. It is a career that requires a high degree of manual skill and I felt that this suited my skill set very much since I had built up a portfolio of henna designs. However, I think it was the work experience placements that I had undertaken that confirmed that I would enjoy and be well suited to a career in dentistry. There is so much variety on a day-to-day basis – I can't imagine I will ever get bored or have a dull day at work!

'Prior to applying, I had managed to undertake placements at the following places: Nechells Dental Clinic (5 days); Fulham Dental Care (5 days); Fine Arts Dental Laboratory (2 days); Acorn Implant and Dental Clinic (3 days) and Walsall Dental Hospital (1 day).

'My placements taught me a wide range of things about the profession. Firstly, I learnt that comforting nervous patients was an integral part of being a great dentist, and the ability to communicate well with patients is key to the success of a treatment. Secondly, placements also showed me the essential qualities needed to make a good dentist, including teamwork between a dentist and their colleagues, excellent communication skills to ensure a good dentist-patient relationship, and manual dexterity. I was fortunate enough to be able to undertake work experience in a variety of dental settings, and it was this that exposed me to the variety that dentistry has to offer and the different specialisms in dentistry such as endodontics and orthodontics.

'The first year of dental school has been really good so far. I have had early clinical exposure and have already administered local anaesthetic to a patient! Academically, I was surprised by how much theory there was to know regarding microbiology and biochemistry, and in this respect it has been extremely difficult to adapt to new teaching styles and be able to recall and understand so much content. I was also surprised at how much focus there is already on anxiety and pain management, which reiterates the need for excellent communication skills to deal with anxious patients.

'So far, I have really enjoyed the clinical aspect of dentistry and being able to learn about things such as periodontology and then applying this in a clinic, whether that be on fellow students or patients. I have also really enjoyed learning neuroanatomy, although at times it has been very difficult.

'I was surprised by the volume of content you were expected to learn, but most of it is quite interesting. The most difficult part of the academic side of university is the new teaching styles you must adapt to. You are expected to do wider reading and revisit lectures you do not understand and it feels like you have to kind of get on with it, with or without the help of lecturers who are often very busy, so you find yourself relying on your peers for extra help.

'My main tip to prospective students is to try to get plenty of work experience in different dental settings because I think it is a good indicator of what dentistry has to offer and whether you would enjoy a career in it.'

3 | Choosing your course

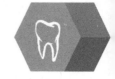

To gain a place at dental school, you have to submit a UCAS application. However, before you do so it is essential that you have thoroughly researched the application process, entrance requirements and the demands of dentistry as a profession. Most people have little understanding of the tasks and challenges that a dentist faces on a day-to-day basis and the career pathways available after graduation. It is therefore vital that you are aware both of what being a dentist entails and of the details of the application process before you consider applying to study dentistry. This will ultimately mean that whatever choice you make it will be a well-informed one.

Choice of school

Once you have completed your work experience and are sure that you want to be a dentist, you need to thoroughly research your choice of dental school.

There are various factors that you should take into account:

- the structure of the course and teaching styles employed
- the academic requirements needed to gain entry to the course
- whether the dental school requires you to sit the UCAT or BMAT
- the location and type of university
- whether the dental school is part of a large university or is a stand-alone medical and dental school.

The majority of information about each university and course can be found on the UCAS website (www.ucas.com) and the individual university websites, so it is well worth spending some time looking here. If you cannot find the answers you need, feel free to call, email, or visit the university open day with any questions relating to admissions or to the course itself. In Chapter 11, there is a list of major dental organisations in the UK that you can contact for further information, and a list of the dental schools and their contact details. What you must remember is that information on websites is always changing, so if you're in doubt it is always best to call the university and speak to someone to get the most up-to-date information.

Remember that when researching different dental courses (and when you come to apply via UCAS), it is vital to make sure that you choose the right course and course code. There are a number of slight variations in the course title and code depending on the type and duration of the course. The five-year undergraduate dentistry course will have the UCAS code A200, A205 or A206, so check this as part of your research.

Apart from talking to current or former dental students or careers advisers, there are a number of other sources of information that will help you in making your choice. There are various independent league tables of dental schools, ranked by a total score that combines several assessment categories, including teaching scores, student–staff ratios and job prospects. For instance, the *Complete University Guide* (www.thecompleteuniversityguide.co.uk) 2019 rankings looked like this:

Table 3 *Complete University Guide* dental school rankings

Rank	University
1st	University of Glasgow
2nd	University of Dundee
3rd	University of Manchester
4th	Newcastle University
5th	Cardiff University
6th	University of Bristol
7th	Queen Mary, University of London
8th	Queen's University Belfast
9th	King's College London
10th	University of Birmingham
11th	University of Leeds
12th	University of Liverpool
13th	University of Aberdeen
14th	University of Sheffield
15th	University of Central Lancashire
16th	University of Plymouth

Source: www.thecompleteuniversityguide.co.uk/league-tables/rankings?s=Dentistry
Reprinted with kind permission from the *Complete University Guide*

Of course, there is no such thing as a bad dental school in the UK, and league tables tell you only a small part of the whole story. They are based on a range of variables and this is why there can be discrepancies between different websites. Remember that league tables are only a guide – they are no substitute for visiting the dental schools, looking at the course content in detail and speaking to those involved with the course.

Open days

Once you have narrowed down the number of dental schools you like to approximately six or seven, you should try to visit them to get a better idea of what studying there will be like. Details of open days can be found on the websites of each university, but sites such as www.open-days.com show details of all open days throughout the year. If you are unable to attend one of the planned open days, it is worth calling the university to see if there are any suitable times when you may be able to look round. Failing this, there is nothing stopping you visiting the university independently to have a casual look around, although it is unlikely that you will be able to see the dental school or talk to members of staff on a visit like this. Do not simply select a dental school because someone has told you that it has a good reputation or that it has a higher number of places available. You will be spending the next five years of your life at one of them, and if you do not like the place you are unlikely to last for the duration. In terms of the particulars of the course, it is vital to visit the dental school itself so that you can listen to any talks being given by the admissions tutors and get a feel for what the department is like. A number of universities may ask you to book a place on the dental admissions talk as there are often limited spaces, so ensure you have looked into this well before you go to the open day. In addition to any general talks being given, you may wish to talk one to one with a representative from the department to ask specific questions. If this is the case, try to have questions prepared so that you can get the most out of this time.

Non-academic considerations

When attending a university open day, there are a number of non-academic points to consider that will give you a better idea of whether the course is for you or not. You should start by considering the university itself – think about the following points:

- location of the university and distance from home: some students prefer to live at home or be very close to home, while others like to get as far away as possible
- campus or city university: again, students seem to have strong preferences about the type of university they study at; some prefer to be in the middle of a big city while others like to be situated on a rural campus, and visiting the university is the only way to get a true feel for its character
- social and sporting facilities: most universities have good sporting facilities, but there will be natural variation in the standard and range of what is available and how far students will have to travel to access these facilities

- accommodation, location and cost: whether the university is a campus or city university will usually have an impact on the location of the accommodation. Usually campus universities will have accommodation on campus or very close by, while city universities will often have it spread out across a wider area. This can have a big impact on the amount of time you spend each day travelling to and from lectures. The quality of accommodation can also vary widely between universities, so it is worth researching the range of different rooms available rather than just the high-end rooms that you are likely to be shown on an open day
- size of the university and student population: although not a major factor for most students, some like the idea of being part of a very large student group, while others prefer smaller universities with a more intimate community.

When you take time to visit a university you will automatically get a feel for these points. From this you should consider whether it is the sort of place where you would like to study. I have worked with many students who think they would like to go to a particular university and then totally change their mind about it after taking the time to visit.

Academic requirements

In addition to the grades they require at A level, most dental schools have specific GCSE requirements too. In summer 2015, the first reformed GCSE specifications were introduced for English language, English literature and mathematics. This was followed by the next batch of subjects in summer 2016, and the remaining batches in summer 2017 and 2018. These subjects are graded from 9 to 1 rather than the A* to G system that has previously been used. The vast majority of students completing their GCSEs in summer 2019 will have completely numerical grades and in summer 2020, all grades will be numerical. As a consequence of the gradual changes, requirements are currently expressed in a combination of numbers and letters but will ultimately move entirely to the numerical system. At this point in time, Ofqual, the examinations regulator, has stated that grade 7 is comparable to an A grade, with grade 8 being roughly equivalent to an A* and grade 9 being above an A*.

Currently, GCSE requirements vary widely from dental school to dental school, but having at least five 7/8 or A/A* grades, with at least 7/A grades in science subjects, English and mathematics will be a significant advantage. In recent years, there have been a number of dental schools that have significantly relaxed their admissions policies in terms of GCSE requirements; however, it still remains a considerable advantage to significantly exceed the minimum requirements they ask for. If your grades fall below these requirements, there is little or no point in applying to that particular course; university admissions tutors often comment on how many applicants they immediately reject because they do not meet the published requirements. If you have genuine extenuating circumstances that explain why you have underachieved (due to illness, family circumstances, etc.), you will need to contact the university to enquire whether they will take this into consideration. In all cases, it is expected that your referee will include in your reference details of the extenuating circumstances that you faced.

In addition to specifying A level grades, some dental schools have previously asked for a minimum grade in any AS subjects you have studied. However, as a consequence of the reforms to A level qualifications, this is now almost a thing of the past. Many schools do not now offer a fourth subject as a separate AS, and so it is the policy of all of the dental schools to ask for only three A level grades.

Another consequence of the A level reforms is that the results from your AS exams now act as stand-alone qualifications instead of contributing to your overall A level grades. So, for example, if you sit AS examinations in biology, chemistry and psychology at the end of your first year of A level study, your marks will not count towards your final A level grades. Different schools have different policies about whether students sit the AS exams at the end of the first year. Although not counting towards your overall A level, these AS grades give admissions tutors a better indication of your academic potential than GCSE grades and A level predictions alone. This means that the first year of A levels is just as important as the second and should not be taken lightly. The typical subject and entry grade requirements are shown in Table 4 on the following pages. Also included in this table are details of GCSE grade and subject requirements.

In the past, a number of dental schools accepted A level students who had not achieved the required grades the first time. Unfortunately, due to the competitive nature of dentistry courses, it is now increasingly unlikely that applications from retake students will have a chance of being successful. There are a few courses that will still consider retake applications, but some will have certain criteria attached. Take the University of Manchester, for example, where retake students can apply, but only if they have already achieved BBB at A level in the first sitting.

Table 4 shows which dental schools consider students who have not achieved the minimum grades at their first attempt. If there have been genuine extenuating circumstances that have caused you to underachieve and you have evidence of this, then it is worth talking to each university to see if they will consider your application, as there can be some leeway here in terms of being considered as a retake student. However, the prevailing conditions are that an increasing number of universities either don't consider extenuating circumstances, such as Plymouth, or require the circumstances to have been reported to the examination boards at the time that the examinations were taken.

Table 4 Dental school admissions policies – 2018/19

University	Standard offer	GCSE requirements	Retakes considered?	Retake offer	Sciences preferred	UCAT policy
Queen's Belfast (A200)	AAA	Minimum C/4 in GCSE Mathematics and English if not offered at AS/A level. GCSE performance in the best 9 subjects will be scored with 4 points awarded for an A*/8 and 3 for an A/7. Points are not awarded for B/6 and C/5.	Yes – if applied to Queen's at first attempt, held an offer as their first choice and achieved AAB at first sitting.	–	Biology/Human Biology and Chemistry	Required
Birmingham (A200)	AAA	Chemistry and Biology at A*/8.	No	–	Chemistry and Biology	Required
Bristol (A206)	AAA (AAC/ABB if certain contextual criteria are considered)	A/7 in GCSE Mathematics and C/5 in GCSE English Language or Literature.	Yes, both GCSE and A level. A maximum of one resit is allowed in any one subject.	–	Chemistry and one of Biology, Physics or Mathematics	Required
Cardiff (A200)	AAA	A/7 in English Language, A/7 in Biology, Chemistry and Physics or AA/77 in double award.	No, unless exceptional extenuating circumstances.	–	Biology and Chemistry at grade A (Critical Thinking and General Studies are excluded)	Required
Dundee (A200)	AAA	Biology, English and Maths to at least GCSE grade B/6 if not studied at A level.	No	–	Chemistry and another science (Biology is recommended, General Studies is not accepted)	Required

Table 4 Continued

University	Standard offer	GCSE requirements	Retakes considered?	Retake offer	Sciences preferred	UCAT policy
Glasgow (A200)	AAA	Six subjects at A/7, must include Mathematics and/or Physics. English language or Literature at B/6.	No	–	Biology and Chemistry	Required
King's (A205)	A*AA + B at AS	At least B/6 in English and Mathematics.	No	–	Biology and Chemistry	Required
Leeds (A200)	AAA	Six at A*–B/6 or above, including Chemistry, Biology (or Dual Science), plus English and Mathematics.	Yes	AAA	Biology and Chemistry	Not required, but BMAT is
Liverpool (A200)	AAA	Minimum of eight, with a minimum of five A/7s and three B/6s. Mathematics, English Language and Science at B/6 or above.	No	–	Biology and Chemistry	Required
Manchester (A206)	AAA	Five at A*/8 or A/7 with B/6 or above in English Language, Mathematics and two science subjects.	Yes – minimum BBB at first sitting.	A*AA with A* in either Biology or Chemistry	Biology and Chemistry	Required

Table 4 Continued

Newcastle (A206)	AAA	No specific requirements.	No	–	Biology and Chemistry	Required
Plymouth (A206)	A*AA – AAA	Seven at A–C/9–4, including English Language, Mathematics and either Single and Additional Science or two from Biology, Chemistry and Physics.	Yes – if achieved ABB at first sitting	A*AA – AAA	Biology and one from Chemistry, Mathematics, Physics and Psychology	Required
Queen Mary (A200)	A*AA	Minimum three A/7s and three B/6s, to include Biology, Chemistry, English Language and Mathematics; the Science Double Award may substitute any individual science.	No	–	Biology or Chemistry and one other science (Chemistry, Biology, Physics or Mathematics)	Required
Sheffield (A200)	AAA	Six at A/7, including Mathematics, English Language and Science.	Yes	AAA	Biology and Chemistry	Required

All information taken from www.ucas.com and from individual university websites.

Another issue to be considered is the requirement to have an A* grade at A level. For entry in 2019, the only courses that openly stated that they would possibly ask for an A* are Manchester, for retake students, King's College, Plymouth and Queen Mary.

The UCAS Tariff

The UCAS tariff system allocates a certain number of points for each qualification achieved. This system allows direct comparison of standards achieved in different qualifications, such as the International Baccalaureate and Scottish Highers, but is mainly used as a tool for universities to report data to the government.

It is worth keeping the details of the tariff in mind if you need to refer to it, but remember that currently all dental offers are made in terms of grades rather than UCAS Tariff points. The Tariff is as follows:

A*	56
A	48
B	40
C	32
D	24
E	16

Other qualifications

If you are not studying A levels, you should check with each dental school about their requirements. The list below offers a rough indication of what they might ask for in a selection of qualifications commonly offered as an alternative to A level study.

- **Scottish Highers:** AAABB–AAAAA at Higher level and two or three subjects at Advanced Higher. Higher level Chemistry and Biology are usually required. Most universities require two to three Advanced Highers, usually including chemistry and biology at grades AA/AAA.
- **International Baccalaureate:** 6, 6, 6 to 6, 6, 7 and 32–38 points overall. Chemistry and biology should be usually taken at Higher level.
- **Cambridge Pre-U:** most universities will accept Cambridge Pre-U qualifications with D3, D3, M3/D3 in the principal subjects. Biology and chemistry will usually be required as two of the principal subjects.
- **BTEC National Diploma:** a few universities are happy to accept this with three Distinctions, but usually only when offered alongside some A level subjects such as chemistry and biology. Once again, it is best to contact the individual universities to discuss their entry requirements.

You will need to check with each university about its specific entry requirements as there is always some variation in their demands. If you have studied qualifications that are not listed here, then you should also check their suitability directly with the university.

Non-dental choices

There are five spaces on the UCAS application, but only four of these can be used to select dentistry courses. Make sure you enter dentistry in all of the four spaces. The remaining space can either be left blank or filled with another course choice. Each university that you apply to will not see the other choices you have made and so you will not be discriminated against because of where else you have applied or what you have entered as your fifth choice. When filling in the final space, you must remember that it will have no impact on your other choices; however, you must also remember that you can write only one personal statement, which is likely to be largely irrelevant in relation to the other subject. So, for example, imagine you applied to four dental schools and then used your fifth space to apply for history. The dental schools you have chosen will not see that you have put history as your fifth choice and so this will not affect their judgement about your commitment to dentistry. However, the history admissions team will see from your personal statement that you are totally committed to dentistry and so is unlikely to make you an offer. In light of this, there are some subjects that are more appropriate to put as your fifth choice, such as biomedical science, and you have a much greater chance of receiving an offer for one of these alongside an offer for dentistry. It can also provide you with another option to follow if you do not secure entry on to a dentistry course or do not achieve the necessary grades, keeping the door open for later graduate entry.

If you do decide to put another science-related course as your fifth choice, you still cannot make your personal statement relevant to more than one subject; keep it entirely focused on dentistry. Any attempt to make it attractive to a number of different admissions tutors in different subjects will adversely affect your chances of making a successful application to dentistry. In some cases though, it may be possible to provide an alternative personal statement directly to the university where your original one is not relevant. Universities are under no obligation to accept this, but it is worth asking them if it is possible prior to applying.

When thinking about which career to pursue, some students consider both dentistry and medicine at some point. If you consider applying for some dentistry and some medicine courses alongside each other, then you are less likely to be successful in securing a place on either course. You should instead decide on one course and put your full effort into preparing a strong application for it, rather than splitting your focus.

4| The UCAS application

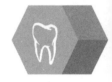

Navigating your way through the UCAS application process can be a daunting process at times. This chapter breaks the process down in order to help you understand each of the stages.

UCAS Apply

When you apply for UK universities, you do so using the UCAS Apply system. The online UCAS form is accessed through the UCAS website (www.ucas.com). You register online either through your school or college, or as a private individual. Some of the information that you provide on the form is factual, such as where you live, where you have studied, what academic qualifications you have, details of examinations that you are going to take, and which university courses you are applying for. Other sections, such as the personal statement and reference, allow more expansive information to be communicated. The sections of the UCAS form are as follows:

- **Personal Details:** this includes all of your basic personal information as well as contact details and details of criminal convictions and any special educational needs.
- **Additional Information:** in this section, you enter details of your ethnicity, parental occupations and details of any activities that you have completed in preparation for higher education.
- **Student Finance:** this section asks about your intention to apply for student finance and if you wish your details to be shared automatically with the student finance organisations.
- **Choices:** this is where you enter your course choices.
- **Education:** this section is used to provide details of all of the schools and colleges you have attended (not including primary school) and the details of the qualifications you have received there.
- **Employment:** in this section, include details of any paid employment.
- **Personal Statement:** this is where you put your personal statement once it is completed.
- **Reference and Predicted Grades:** finally, this is where your academic referee enters their reference about you and the grades you have been predicted for each subject.

Once your form is complete, it is accessed by the person who will write your reference; they then check it, add the reference and predicted grades and send it to UCAS. Remember, that when you have completed your form and press 'send', the form does not go straight to UCAS, but is instead sent to the person who oversees the UCAS process at your school or college. This means that your form can be returned to you at this point if there are any mistakes that need correcting. If you register as a private individual, a request for your reference will be sent to the person you have nominated as your referee. You will only be able to send your form to UCAS once this has been completed.

Once your application has been submitted, you can keep track of the responses from the universities using UCAS Track.

When to submit your UCAS application

The closing date for receipt of the application by UCAS is 15 October. Remember that this is the deadline by which the form is required to be submitted to UCAS and so your school or college will most likely have an earlier deadline so it can get your reference written. This will probably be around two weeks earlier. Late applications are accepted by UCAS, but the dental schools are not obliged to consider them; because of the pressure on places, it is unlikely that late applications will be considered. You can submit your application at any time between the beginning of September and 15 October. As long as you don't miss the October deadline, your application will receive the same treatment, regardless of when it is submitted. However, in terms of your own peace of mind, it is always recommended to submit as early as you can.

The safest bet for getting your application completed and sent as soon as possible is to make a start on it in the first year of your A levels. Start researching the different universities and the different courses as soon as possible and then begin writing your personal statement and get feedback on it. Ultimately, you want to be in a position where you have a final draft of your personal statement and all of your choices sorted by the beginning of September in your final year of A levels.

The reference

As well as your GCSE results, personal statement and predicted grades, the admissions team will take into account your academic reference. This is where your headteacher, housemaster or housemistress or head of sixth form writes about your academic potential and personal attributes. The referee is expected to be as honest as possible, and to try to accurately assess your character and potential. You may believe that you have all of the qualities – academic and personal – necessary in a dentist, but unless you have demonstrated these to your teachers, they may not be able to support your application.

Ideally, your efforts to impress them will have begun at the start of the sixth form (or preferably before this); you will have become involved in school activities, while at the same time working hard on your A level subjects and developing strong interpersonal skills, demonstrated by your interactions with staff and students. If you do not feel as though you have done this, don't worry, because it is never too late. Some people mature later than others, so if this does not sound like you, start to make efforts to get involved in the wider life of your school or college, as this will help provide evidence for the people who will contribute to your reference.

As part of the reference, your referee will need to predict the grades that you are likely to achieve. As Table 4 in Chapter 3 (see pages 37–39) shows, the most likely minimum requirement for entry is AAA, although King's College, Plymouth, Queen Mary and Manchester (for retake students) indicate that they may include an A* as part of the offer. If your predicted grades are lower than this, it is unlikely that you will be considered. Talk to your teachers and find out whether you are on target for these grades. If not, you need to do one or all of the following:

- work harder or more effectively, and make sure that your teachers notice that you are doing so
- get some extra help either at school or outside: for instance, an Easter revision course
- delay submitting your UCAS application until you have your A level results.

UCAT

All but one of the UK dental schools (Leeds) now require applicants to sit the pre-admissions test known as the UCAT (the University Clinical Aptitude Test) before they apply. (This was previously known as the UKCAT.) This test is designed to help discriminate between the many highly qualified applicants who apply for dentistry courses each year. It is important to note that the UCAT is **not** based on science content from your A level science subjects, but on assessing your skills and attributes.

Registration for the UCAT usually opens at the beginning of May of the year you submit your UCAS form and closes in the middle of September. Testing then starts at the beginning of July and finishes at the start of October. It is vital to consult the UCAT website (www.ukcat.ac.uk) for the exact registration and testing dates for the year you are applying, so that you know precisely what you need to do and when.

The first step is to register on the UCAT website. You will be asked to select the test centre where you wish to sit the test and then the date and time. At the start of May you should try to register as early as possible in order to get your preferred date and location; there are a number of students each year who have to travel great distances to find a test centre that still has spaces. If you have any disabilities or additional needs that require you to have extra time in examinations, you should ensure that you register for the UKCATSEN instead of the regular test. If you require special access arrangements for examinations, then you should contact Pearson VUE customer services directly to discuss these arrangements before you book the test. The customer service UCAT helpline is 0161 855 7409 and lines are open from 8am to 5pm (UK time), Monday to Friday, excluding bank holidays.

It is vital to take the test before you submit your application so that you can make an informed decision about which universities to apply to. For example, if you apply to universities that put a lot of emphasis on a high UCAT score and then you underperform in the test, it will reduce your chances of a successful application. It is also advisable not to take the test too early. As much time as possible is needed for preparation, so if you sit the test at the beginning of July, you are unlikely to have had the chance to carry out all the preparation needed.

The cost for those taking the test in 2018 was £65 for candidates taking the test in the EU before 31 August, £87 for candidates taking the test in the EU between 1 September and 3 October and £115 for candidates taking the test outside of the EU. There are some bursaries available to students who may struggle to meet the cost of the test; these can be applied for through the UCAT website.

The test itself is sat at an external centre in the location you have chosen. You should aim to arrive at least 15 minutes before your test time, remembering to take a printout of the email confirming your registration and one piece of approved photographic ID, such as a passport or driving licence. It is important to remember that you must arrive on time for the slot you have booked; if you fail to do so, you will simply not be able to take the test and will have to rebook for a later date and pay the test fee again. The test is entirely computer-based, lasts for two hours and consists of the following five sections:

1. verbal reasoning
2. decision making
3. quantitative reasoning
4. abstract reasoning
5. situational judgement.

The structure and layout of each section are described below.

1. Verbal reasoning

This section is 22 minutes long (1 minute for reading instructions, 21 minutes' test time) and contains 44 questions, which are known as items. The UCAT website states that this section 'assesses your ability to read and think carefully about information presented in passages and to determine whether specific conclusions can be drawn from information presented'. In this section, you will be presented with 11 short passages of text each with four associated items (questions).

There are two types of question in this section. Type one presents you with a statement related to the passage and then asks you to deduce if the statement is 'true', 'false' or 'can't tell', based on the information you are given in the passage. The second type of question provides you with a question or incomplete statement which has four possible options to complete it. You must choose the most suitable response.

2. Decision making

This section is 32 minutes long (1 minute for reading instructions, 31 minutes' test time) and contains 29 items (questions). The UCAT website states that it 'tests your ability to apply logic to reach a decision or conclusion, evaluate arguments and analyse statistical information'.

In this section you will be presented with text, charts, tables, graphs or diagrams and a single question relating to each one. All questions are separate and do not share data. Some questions have four answers where only one is correct. Other questions will require you to respond 'yes' or 'no' to each of the five statements.

3. Quantitative reasoning

This section is 25 minutes long (1 minute for reading instructions, 24 minutes' test time) and contains 36 items (questions). The UCAT website states that it 'assesses your ability to use numerical skills to solve problems. Questions are less to do with numerical facility and more to do with problem solving'.

In this section, you will be presented with tables, charts and/or graphs and then be asked to answer related questions. Some data sets have four related questions and some are completely standalone. Each question has five possible answers to choose from.

4. Abstract reasoning

This section is 14 minutes long (1 minute for reading instructions, 13 minutes' test time) and contains 55 items (questions). The UCAT website states that it 'assesses your ability to identify patterns amongst abstract shapes where irrelevant and distracting material may lead to incorrect conclusions. The test therefore measures your ability to change track, critically evaluate and generate hypotheses and requires you to query judgements as you go along'.

In this section there are four question categories and you will be presented with all of these types. The different types of questions are:

Type 1: You are given two different sets of shapes which are labelled set A and set B. For each question you are given another shape and asked to work out whether it belongs to set A, set B or neither set.

Type 2: You are given a set of shapes that follow in series one after another. You then have to choose which shape would come next.

Type 3: You are given a written statement and then have to decide which shape completes the statement.

Type 4: You are presented with a set A and set B of shapes and have to select which of four options belongs to set A or B.

5. Situational judgement

This section is 27 minutes long (1 minute for reading instructions, 26 minutes' test time) and contains 69 questions associated with 20 scenarios. The UCAT website states that it 'measures capacity to understand real world situations and to identify critical factors and appropriate behaviour in dealing with them'.

A series of scenarios are presented to you, each with an associated set of between two and five questions. The first type of questions can ask you to rate the appropriateness of particular responses to the given scenario, while the second type requires you to rate the importance of particular responses to the scenarios.

For the **appropriateness** questions, you are required to choose from the following options:

- a very appropriate thing to do
- appropriate, but not ideal
- inappropriate, but not awful
- a very inappropriate thing to do.

For the **importance** questions, you choose from the following options:

- very important
- important
- of minor importance
- not important at all.

This section is scored separately from the initial sections and is not given a numerical score; instead, you are assigned a band which relates to the strength of responses that you have given. You can be placed in band 1, 2, 3 or 4, with band 1 representing an 'excellent' performance, band 2 representing a 'good' performance, band 3 representing a 'modest' performance and band 4 representing a 'low' performance.

While it is not possible to revise for the UCAT, students find that the more practice they have had on UCAT-style questions, the better prepared they feel and the better they perform. The UCAT website (www.ukcat.ac.uk/ukcat-test/ukcat-preparation) is an invaluable source of information; there is an official guide to the test, a bank of 400 questions, a number of practice tests and other resources. There are also numerous books available that offer hints, tips and practice questions; it is worth flicking through the various titles in a bookshop to see which is best suited to your needs, but remember that none of these books is authorised or written by UCAT itself.

The biggest challenge you will face while taking the test is lack of time because there are so many questions to answer in such a short period. It is vital for you to use the practice tests to get a feel for what it is like to be in a time-pressured situation and to understand how long you can spend on each question in each section.

Tips for UCAT

- You cannot revise, but you can prepare. There is no scientific content to memorise, but knowing the structure of the test and what the questions look like will help you to maximise your performance on the day.
- Brush up on your basic maths skills. Good mental arithmetic will make your life a lot easier when answering questions related to data or calculations.
- Practice reading news articles that you are unfamiliar with to improve your ability to read and understand passages of text when under time pressure. One of the biggest challenges for students is meeting the demands of reading lots of information in the Verbal Reasoning section, so any practice at this will help you to prepare.
- The test is purposely difficult and time pressured. Don't panic when you don't know an answer and when you run out of time. These are both inevitable consequences of the test and are designed to see how you perform under pressure.
- Guess answers where needed. There is no negative marking on any section, so if you do not know the answer, try to eliminate obviously incorrect answers first. If you have no idea, a random guess is better than a blank space.
- Attempt all of the official practice questions to familiarise yourself with the style and timing of each section. This is also vital so that you get used to being tested on a computer screen and can deal with all of the difficulties that this brings.

Sample questions from each subtest follow, courtesy of Kaplan Test Prep.

UCAT Verbal Reasoning Practice Questions

Subtest length: 44 questions (11 sets of 4 questions)
Subtest timing: 21 minutes (2 minutes per set)
Sample length: 4 questions
Sample timing: 2 minutes

In September 1997, Scotland held a referendum on the question of devolution. Over 60 per cent of eligible voters went to the polls, and they voted in favour of both questions on the ballot-paper. On the first question, asking whether there should be a Scottish Parliament, 74.3 per cent of voters agreed, including a majority in favour in every Scottish local authority area. On the second question, asking whether that Parliament should have tax-varying powers, 63.5 per cent of voters agreed, including a majority in favour in every Scottish local authority area except Orkney and Dumfries & Galloway. In response to the results of this referendum, the UK Parliament passed the 1998 Scotland Act, which was given Royal Assent on 19 November 1998. The first members of Scottish Parliament (MSPs) were elected on 6 May 1999, and the Queen formally opened the Scottish Parliament on 1 July 1999, at which time it took up its full powers.

Under the terms of the 1998 Scotland Act, the Scottish Parliament has the authority to pass laws that affect Scotland on a range of issues. These issues are known as 'devolved matters', as power in these matters has been transferred (or 'devolved') from a national body (the UK Parliament at Westminster) to regional bodies (the Scottish Parliament, the National Assembly for Wales, and the Northern Ireland Assembly). Education, Agriculture, Justice, and Health (including NHS issues in Scotland) are among the issues devolved to the Scottish Parliament. The Scottish Parliament also has the power to set the basic rate of income tax, as high as 3 pence to the pound.

The 1998 Scotland Act also provides for 'reserved matters', which Scots must take up through their MPs at Westminster rather than through their MSPs. Such reserved matters, on which the Scottish Parliament cannot pass legislation, include Foreign Affairs, Defence, and National Security.

In Scottish parliamentary elections, each voter has two votes: one vote for the MSP for their local constituency, and one vote for the candidate or party to represent their Scottish Parliamentary Region. There are 73 local constituencies, and 8 Scottish Parliamentary Regions; each local constituency is represented by one local MSP, and each region is represented by 7 regional MSPs. These local and regional MSPs account for the total membership of the Scottish Parliament. Thus, every Scotsman or Scotswoman is represented by a total of 8 MSPs (1 local and 7 regional).

1. In the 1997 referendum, more voters in Dumfries & Galloway were in favour of a Scottish Parliament than were in favour of tax-varying powers for a Scottish Parliament.

A.   True
B.   False
C.   Can't tell

2. The Scottish Parliament can raise the basic rate of income tax by 3 pence to the pound.

A.   True
B.   False
C.   Can't tell

3. NHS issues in Wales are among the issues devolved to the National Assembly for Wales.

A.   True
B.   False
C.   Can't tell

4. There are a total of 129 MSPs in the Scottish Parliament.

A.   True
B.   False
C.   Can't tell

UCAT Decision Making Practice Questions

Subtest length: 29 questions (individual items, rather than sets)
Subtest timing: 31 minutes (1 minute per question)
Sample length: 3 questions
Sample timing: 3 minutes

A queue at a corner shop consists of four people: Hamza, Iris, Johnny and Kenzie. Each person is buying a different item, including drinks (milk, wine) and snacks (ice cream, biscuits).

The person buying biscuits is standing somewhere between Hamza and the person buying wine.

Iris isn't buying a drink.

Johnny is standing directly behind the person buying milk.

Kenzie isn't at the front of the queue.

1. Which of the following must be true?

A.   Hamza is buying ice cream.
B.   Iris is standing between Hamza and Johnny.
C.   Johnny is buying biscuits.
D.   Kenzie is standing directly behind Iris.

2. Should it be illegal to eat any meat from animals or any animal products, like milk or eggs?

A.   Yes, because there are health risks associated with eating too much red meat.

B.   Yes, because we are running out of resources to support the meat demands of our rapidly growing population.

C.   No, because there are some essential nutrients that are difficult to obtain in sufficient quantity without eating meat or animal products.

D.   No, because it is not the role of government to pass laws affecting the food supply.

3.   All my books are novels. Some of your books are non-fiction, but none of your books are biographies. This book is either yours or mine.

        Place 'Yes' if the conclusion does follow. Place 'No' if the conclusion does not follow.

This book is a biography.	
This book is not non-fiction.	
If this book is mine, it is a novel.	
If this book is not yours, it could be a biography.	
If this book is not mine, it is not a biography.	

UCAT Quantitative Reasoning Practice Questions

Subtest length: 36 questions (9 sets of 4 questions)
Subtest timing: 24 minutes (2 minutes per set)
Sample length: 4 questions
Sample timing: 2 minutes

The total cost of hiring certain types of helicopters for certain numbers of hours is given in the table. Total cost equals the deposit plus the hourly rate per hour for the number of hours required. Some information has been omitted from the table.

Type	Hours	Deposit	Hourly Rate	Total Cost
A	3	£120	£225	£795
B	5	£300	—	£2,500
C	6	—	£495	£3,300
D	7	£575	£525	—
E	10	—	£575	£6,750

1. Andre's total cost of hiring a Type D helicopter was £2,675. What was the total time (in hours) for which he hired the helicopter?

A. 2
B. 3
C. 4
D. 5
E. 6

2. If the deposit for Type E helicopters increases by 30% on Saturdays, what is the total cost of hiring a Type E helicopter for 3 hours on a Saturday?

A. £1,914.00
B. £2,322.50
C. £2,602.50
D. £3,025.00
E. £3,600.00

3. Rupali hired a Type B helicopter for 2 hours on Thursday and a Type A helicopter for 6 hours on Friday. By how much does Rupali's total cost of renting a helicopter increase from Thursday to Friday?

A. 14.36%
B. 24.58%
C. 34.75%
D. 44.86%
E. 54.95%

4. The total cost of hiring a Type F helicopter is £1,430 per hour. If Type F helicopters have the same deposit as Type C helicopters, what is the ratio of the hourly rate for a Type C helicopter to the hourly rate for a Type F helicopter?

A. 9:20
B. 12:25
C. 21:40
D. 15:26
E. 9:14

UCAT Abstract Reasoning Practice Questions

Subtest length: 55 questions (11 sets of 5 questions)
Subtest timing: 13 minutes (1 minute per set)
Sample length: 5 questions
Sample timing: 1 minute

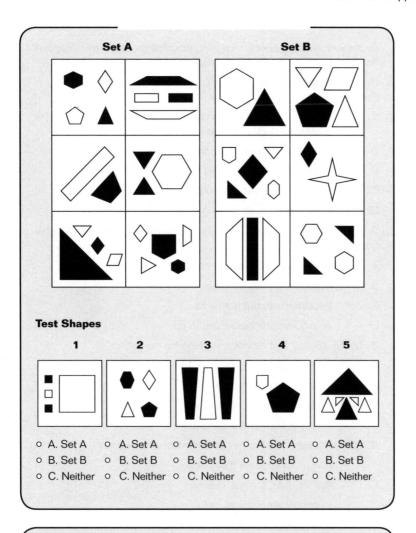

Set A   **Set B**

Test Shapes

1   2   3   4   5

- ○ A. Set A
- ○ B. Set B
- ○ C. Neither

- ○ A. Set A
- ○ B. Set B
- ○ C. Neither

- ○ A. Set A
- ○ B. Set B
- ○ C. Neither

- ○ A. Set A
- ○ B. Set B
- ○ C. Neither

- ○ A. Set A
- ○ B. Set B
- ○ C. Neither

UCAT Situational Judgement Practice Questions

Subtest length: 20 scenarios, 2 to 5 questions each (69 questions total)

Subtest timing: 26 minutes (20–30 seconds per scenario, then 10–15 seconds per question)

Sample length: 4 questions

Sample timing: 1 minute

During a busy weekend on call, Jagdeep, a first year junior doctor, is called to see Mr Morley, an elderly patient on the ward, who is complaining of a headache. Jagdeep has never met Mr Morley before. On his arrival at the patient's bed, Mr Morley takes one look at Jagdeep and states that he does not look old enough to be a doctor. Mr Morley says he should send someone more qualified instead. Jagdeep knows his seniors are busy seeing sick patients on other wards, and Jagdeep has many other tasks he must complete before the end of his shift.

How **appropriate** are each of the following responses by Jagdeep in this situation?

1. Tell Mr Morley that he can examine him now or he will likely not be seen by another doctor for a few hours.

A.   A very appropriate thing to do

B.   Appropriate, but not ideal

C.   Inappropriate, but not awful

D.   A very inappropriate thing to do

2. Ask Mr Morley how old he thinks he is whilst having a read of his notes.

A.   A very appropriate thing to do

B.   Appropriate, but not ideal

C.   Inappropriate, but not awful

D.   A very inappropriate thing to do

3. Tell Mr Morley that he does not look his age either.

A.   A very appropriate thing to do

B.   Appropriate, but not ideal

C.   Inappropriate, but not awful

D.   A very inappropriate thing to do

4. Tell Mr Morley he will send another doctor to see him.

A.   A very appropriate thing to do

B.   Appropriate, but not ideal

C.   Inappropriate, but not awful

D.   A very inappropriate thing to do

Practice questions provided by Kaplan Test Prep, a leading provider of preparation for the UCAT and BMAT. See www.kaptest.co.uk.

Verbal Reasoning Practice Questions - Answers

1. (A)

2. (B)

3. (C)

4. (A)

Decision Making Practice Questions - Answers

1. (D)
2. (C)
3. NO; NO; YES; NO; YES

Quantitative Reasoning Practice Questions - Answers

1. (C)
2. (D)
3. (B)
4. (A)

Abstract Reasoning Practice Questions - Answers

1. (A)
2. (C)
3. (C)
4. (A)
5. (B)

Situational Judgement Practice Questions - Answers

1. (A)
2. (B)
3. (D)
4. (D)

Answer explanations for each practice question can be found on Kaplan's web site at www.kaptest.co.uk/ukcat/practice-questions.

BMAT

The BioMedical Admissions Test (BMAT) is an alternative admissions test that is used for a relatively small number of dental, medical and biomedical science courses at selected universities. Currently, only the University of Leeds requires students that apply for dentistry to sit the test. BMAT currently has two dates that it can be completed. The first sitting is carried out at the start of September and the second at the end of October. As it stands, all universities apart from Oxford accept results from either sitting.

If you are taking the BMAT, your school or college will need to register you for the test by 6pm (UK time) on 12 August for the September sitting or 6pm (UK time) on 15 October for the October sitting.

The BMAT is a very different prospect to the UCAT; it is a written test that is conducted at your school or college like any GCSE or A-level exam. The test consists of three sections and lasts for two hours in total. Students are advised that it tests both skills and knowledge and as a consequence does require some study. As with the UCAT, it is worth spending as much time as you can preparing for it so that you know exactly what to expect. The BMAT website (www.admissionstesting. org/for-test-takers/bmat/bmat-october or www.admissionstesting.org/ for-test-takers/bmat/bmat-september) provides comprehensive information about the structure of the test, guidance on preparing for the test, as well as details of the scientific content that will be tested. There is also a number of practice papers included that will help you to get used to the question style and format as well as the timing of each of the sections. There are also numerous other websites and preparation course providers that provide useful practice materials and support.

The three sections of the test are as follows:

1. aptitude and skills
2. scientific knowledge and applications
3. writing task.

The structure and layout of each section is described below.

1. Aptitude and Skills

The Aptitude and Skills section lasts for one hour and consists of 35 multiple-choice questions. The test is designed to demonstrate your ability to solve problems, understand arguments, analyse data and make inferences. This part of the test is very similar in style to UCAT and uses the same sorts of skills as the verbal, quantitative and abstract reasoning sections.

BMAT® Aptitude & Skills Practice Questions

Have a go at the below sample BMAT Aptitude and Skills practice questions, taken from the full set.

DIRECTIONS (for full test):

Answer every question. Points are awarded for correct answers only. There are no penalties for incorrect answers.

All questions are worth 1 mark.

3. Media coverage of organ donation has increased as the Government considers making the donor registry 'opt-out', rather than 'opt-in'. Every week, newspapers and TV reports are filled with grim stories and statistics of waiting lists and deaths of those waiting for a transplant. Regardless of any changes to legislation, the media could do more to increase organ donation at present. For example, the frequent news reports on the need for more donated organs rarely mention how, exactly, members of the public can 'opt-in' to the donor registry. This practice stands in stark contrast to the presentation of such stories in other countries, such as the USA and Canada, where stories on the need for more organ donors almost always end with contact details for joining the donor registry. Providing viewers with a phone number or website for joining the registry is seen as a public service, part of the media's responsibility in calling attention to such a problem.

Which of the following best summarises the main conclusion of the argument?

A It's easier to become an organ donor in the USA or Canada than in the UK.

B Sometimes the media can help to solve the problems it identifies.

C The Government wants to make organ donation compulsory.

D Many people die waiting for organs each year as there are too few donors opting-in to the registry.

E Everyone should be required to join the organ donor registry.

4. Shannon and Dave are hosting a dinner party for six friends. The surface of the dining table is circular, with chairs set out equal distances around its circumference, as shown below. Each chair is directly opposite one other chair.

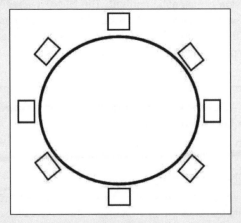

Dave prefers to sit directly opposite Shannon. Rachael and James are a couple, and prefer to sit next to each other. Ben fancies Lola, and he's a bit shy, so he prefers to sit directly opposite her. Dave and Shannon can't stand Patrick, whom Cindy is seeing, so neither of them will sit next to him.

If the seating plan meets everyone's preferences, what is the probability that Cindy will be seated directly opposite Rachael?

A 1/16

B 1/12

C 1/6

D 1/2

Practice questions provided by Kaplan Test Prep, a leading provider of preparation for the UCAT and BMAT. See www.kaptest.co.uk/courses/uk-university/bmat/practice-questions/ bmat-prep-tools, then enter your details to receive your Free BMAT Starter Kit via email.

Answers

3. B

4. D

Answer explanations for each question can be found in Kaplan's Free BMAT Starter Kit using the above link.

2. Scientific Knowledge

The Scientific Knowledge section lasts for 30 minutes and consists of 27 multiple-choice questions. This section tests your ability to apply GCSE-standard scientific knowledge and, as such, requires a knowledge of biology, chemistry, physics and mathematics. This marks a departure from the skills required for UCAT and is the only section that requires revision of scientific content. The BMAT website provides an electronic 'revision' guide to allow candidates to prepare the basics needed for this section (www.admissionstestingservice.org/for-test-takers/bmat/preparing-for-bmat/section-2-preparation).

BMAT® Scientific Knowledge and Applications Practice Questions

Have a go at the below sample BMAT Scientific Knowledge and Applications practice questions, taken from the full set.

DIRECTIONS (for full test):

Answer every question. Points are awarded for correct answers only. There are no penalties for incorrect answers. All questions are worth 1 mark. Some questions have more than 1 correct answer. Read carefully to ensure that you select the appropriate number of answers. Calculators are not permitted during any portion of the test.

1. Haemophilia B (Christmas disease) is an X-linked recessive disorder. Both Jane's father and maternal grandfather suffer from Haemophilia B.

Which of Jane's relatives is neither a carrier of, nor suffers from, Christmas disease?

A Her sister

B Her father's monozygotic twin

C Her maternal uncle

D Her maternal aunt

E Her paternal grandmother

3. Three points in the (x, y) coordinate plane lie at:

(a, b)

$(a+3\sqrt{2}, b)$

$(a+\sqrt{2}, b-4\sqrt{2})$

What is the area of the triangle described by these coordinates?

A $\sqrt{2}$

B 6

C $5\sqrt{2}$

D 12

E $12\sqrt{2}$

Practice questions provided by Kaplan Test Prep, a leading provider of preparation for the UCAT and BMAT. See www.kaptest.co.uk/courses/uk-university/bmat/practice-questions/ bmat-prep-tools, then enter your details to receive your Free BMAT Starter Kit via email.

Answers

1. C

3. D

Answer explanations for each question can be found in Kaplan's Free BMAT Starter Kit using the above link.

3. Writing Task

The final stage is the Writing Task, which lasts for 30 minutes and requires you to choose one task from a possible three questions. This is predominantly designed to see how you can arrange your ideas and then communicate them in written form. There are strict limits on the amount of space available, so one of the main purposes of this section is to test your ability to write clearly and concisely and get your points across without waffling,

BMAT® Writing Practice Questions

Time: 30 MINUTES

Have a go at the writing practice questions, taken from the full set. Here we show two of the four essay title options.

DIRECTIONS (for full test):

Answer only one task from the choice of four essay titles. You must write your answer by hand, and are limited to a space consisting of one side of A4. You are permitted to make any preparatory notes as needed, but time spent on such notes counts against the 30 minutes allowed for the essay. In this task, you are expected to show how well you can order and explore ideas, and convey these ideas in clear, effective writing. You may not use dictionaries or any other reference books or resources. Essays are assigned a numerical score. To achieve a top mark, you must address all aspects of the question and write compellingly with few errors in logic or in use of English.

1. A scientific man ought to have no wishes, no affections – a mere heart of stone. Charles Darwin

Write an essay in which you address the following points:

Why should those who practise science or medicine have 'no wishes, no affections'? What is the negative impact when scientists or doctors have 'hearts of stone'? How could a scientist or doctor best reconcile these competing concerns?

2. The greatest enemy of knowledge is not ignorance; it is the illusion of knowledge. Stephen Hawking

Write an essay in which you address the following points:

In science, how is the illusion of knowledge an enemy of knowledge? Can you argue that ignorance is itself an enemy of knowledge? By what criteria could you assess the comparative impact of these two, to determine which is the greater enemy of scientific knowledge?

Practice questions provided by Kaplan Test Prep, a leading provider of preparation for the UCAT and BMAT. See www.kaptest.co.uk/courses/uk-university/bmat/practice-questions/bmat-prep-tools, then enter your details to receive your Free BMAT Starter Kit via email.

Answer explanations for each question can be found in Kaplan's Free BMAT Starter Kit using the above link.

Tips for BMAT

- Revise. You must get to grips with GCSE-standard theory for biology, chemistry, physics and mathematics. This is more of a challenge in the subjects that you haven't studied so far at A level.

- Become familiar with the structure of each section by completing the past papers available. This will also help you to become familiar with the time available.
- As with the UCAT, limited time is one of the biggest problems with the test. Try to get as far through the test as you can and guess the answers to any remaining questions.
- Don't leave any blanks. If you don't know the answer, try to eliminate obviously incorrect ones first. If you can't eliminate any answers, a random guess is better than no answer at all.
- In sections 1 and 2, there is no negative marking, so incorrect answers will not be penalised. Section 3 carries a mark for the quality of written English, so try to write as clearly as you can.
- Don't panic. The test is designed to be challenging, so it is vital that you are philosophical about questions you do not know the answer to: just do your best and move on to the next question.

Deferred entry

Some admissions tutors may be happy to consider students who take a gap year; however, if you are considering following this route, you first need to make sure that you contact your prospective universities in order to see if they would be willing to accept a deferral. If you receive positive feedback about this route, the next step is to ensure that you have plans in place to use the time constructively. A year spent watching daytime TV is not going to impress anybody, whereas independent travelling, charity or voluntary work either at home or abroad, work experience or a responsible job will all indicate that you have used the time to develop independence and maturity.

Having a job during your gap year in somewhere like a shop or a bar may seem like a good idea and is certainly better than sitting around doing nothing all the time; however, if you wish to demonstrate your ongoing commitment to pursuing dentistry as a career, then you should concentrate on getting further experience in a job or placement directly related to the field.

You can either apply for deferred entry when you submit your UCAS application, in which case you need to outline your plans clearly in your personal statement, or apply in September following the publication of your A level results. If you expect to be predicted the right grades, and the feedback from your school or college is that you will be given a good reference, you should apply for deferred entry. On the other hand, if you are advised by your referee that you are unlikely to be considered, you should give yourself more time to work with your referees by waiting until you have your A level results.

Dental timeline

Figure 1 opposite shows what you will need to be aware of over the course of your A level studies and gives an overview of the timings of some of the various tasks that you should plan for if you are to maximise your chances of gaining entry into a dental school.

As you can see, your main task in year 12 is to start researching your courses and options, organising and carrying out work experience and then preparing your personal statement. The summer between year 12 and year 13 should be used to continue building your work experience as well as registering and preparing for the UCAT. In year 13 you must hit the ground running, because the UCAT and your UCAS application must be finished by early October. At the same time, you must also ensure that you stay on top of your studies so you maximise your chances of achieving the A grades you will need, and you should also start preparing for interview and practising your interview skills. Once your final exams are finished at the end of the year, it is simply a matter of waiting for your results so you can see whether you have secured a place.

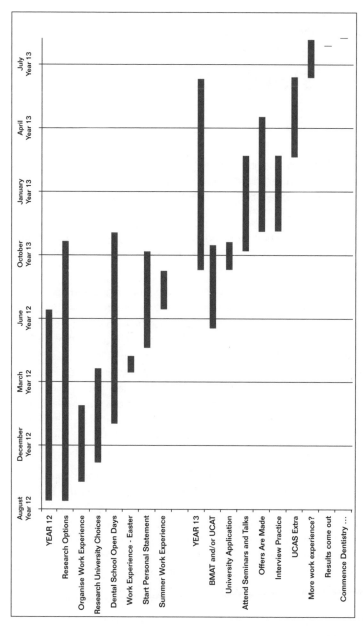

Figure 1 Timeline to guide your application to study dentistry

5 | Personal statement

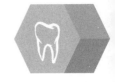

In spite of the decline in application numbers for dentistry in recent years, the demand is still extremely high when compared to most other undergraduate courses. So what exactly is the impact of sustained high demand for places?

Firstly there is a continued requirement for very high A level grades, but, alongside this, there is an increased level of scrutiny of all the other elements of your application.

Your application is likely to be received by the university and considered along with many others at the same time. On average, a dental school may receive in excess of 700 applications and have to select around 300 applicants to be called for interview. Of those who apply, there will be some who are automatically rejected as they do not fulfil all the entry criteria; for example, not meeting the GCSE grade requirements. Following this, it is down to the admissions team to try to select whom to interview from the remaining candidates. Many of the applicants who are still being considered at this stage will have excellent GCSE profiles, outstanding predicted A level grades and a strong UCAT (or BMAT, in the case of Leeds) performance. So how do the selectors make their choices?

When it comes to distinguishing between highly qualified candidates, one of the most important factors that is considered is the personal statement. If this is badly worded, littered with errors or lacking detail about the attributes and experiences of the candidate, your application will stand a chance of being rejected without being taken further. Ultimately, this means that the more thought that you give to your UCAS application and personal statement, the better they will be and the greater your chance of being asked to come in for an interview and being made a conditional offer. Remember that the selectors will not know about the things that you have forgotten to say: they can get an impression of you only from what is in the application. I have come across many good students who never secured an interview simply because their personal statement did not adequately reflect their skills and experience.

Note that only a small proportion of applicants will be interviewed, so while it's important to prepare for the interview it's vital that you make your personal statement and overall application as strong as it possibly can be to maximise the chance of you being called to interview in the first place.

The following sections will tell you more about what the selectors are look-ing for in a personal statement, and how you can avoid common mistakes.

Personal statement basics

When constructing your personal statement, there are several impor-tant things that you need to consider. First, your personal statement needs to be no more than 47 lines or 4,000 characters, including spaces; this is a strict limit and so you need to ensure that you are as close to this as possible. You must then consider the key themes of your personal statement, which are:

- why you want to be a dentist
- what you have done to gain work experience and voluntary work placements
- what experiences have particularly stood out to you and why
- what your academic interests are and how these have furthered your desire to pursue dentistry
- what you have done to develop the skills needed to become a dentist
- what you have done outside of academic studies to develop your skills.

The personal statement is your opportunity to demonstrate to the selec-tors that you are fully committed to studying dentistry and have the right motivation and personal qualities to do so successfully. A typical per-sonal statement takes time and effort to get right: don't expect perfec-tion after one draft. At each stage of the process you should take time to read through your statement, and ask yourself the question: 'Does it sound like me?' If not, redraft it. You should also take the time to get your academic advisers or teachers to give you feedback at each stage; this will ensure you stay on the right track.

Sections of the personal statement

Why dentistry?

This should be your first section and will outline to the admissions tutors your motivation for wanting to study dentistry. A high proportion of UCAS applications contain stock phrases such as: 'From an early age I have wanted to be a dentist because it is the only career that combines my love of science with the chance to work with people.' Not only do admissions tutors get bored with reading such statements, remarks like these are also clearly untrue: if you think about it, there are many careers that combine science and working with people, including medi-cine, teaching, pharmacy, physiotherapy and nursing. Nevertheless, the basic idea of this sentence may well apply to you. If so, you need to personalise it. You could mention an incident that first got you interested in dentistry – a visit to your own dentist, a conversation with a family friend, a talk or lesson at school or something you witnessed during your work experience, for instance. You should also ensure that you avoid giving reasons relating to money or status; any mention of wanting to be a dentist so that you can earn £200,000 a year is an almost guaranteed way of being rejected!

It is a common misconception that you need to begin your personal statement with an inspirational quotation or grand statement; again, admissions tutors get bored of students trying to squeeze in lines from books, poems or films that have no real meaning to the applicant. What an admissions tutor would rather see is a statement of the genuine reasons why you want to study dentistry, written in clear, uncomplicated English.

Another common pitfall in the first paragraph is taking up valuable space with an explanation about what the subject is about or what the profession entails. For example: 'Dentistry is a highly regarded profession that requires a high degree of manual dexterity and attention to detail.' Remember that the people reading your statement know exactly what the profession is about and so do not need to be lectured on it! Instead, you need to take the time to explain about your own interest in the profession and why you feel compelled to follow this career path.

What work experience and voluntary work have you undertaken?

This section is important to demonstrate that you gained something from your work experience and voluntary placements, and that they have given you an insight into the profession. Start by talking about your dental-specific experiences. You should give an indication of the length of time you spent at each placement and the impressions you gained. You could comment on what aspects of dentistry attract you, on what you found interesting, or on something that you hadn't expected. But remember that this is not a shopping list; you are not simply reeling off experience after experience; you are expected to provide deeper reflection about what you have seen.

Beyond this, you should also mention any other work experience or voluntary work you have had in a caring or clinical role and what you learned from it. Although you may not think of these sorts of experiences as being relevant, they can often demonstrate to an admissions tutor good interpersonal skills or commitment and dedication.

Here is a sample description of a student's work experience that would probably not impress the admissions team.

'I spent three days at my local dental practice. I saw some patients having fillings, and a man whose false teeth didn't fit. It was very interesting.'

In contrast, the example below would be much more convincing because it is clear that the student was interested in what was happening.

> *'During my two weeks at the Smith and Smith Dental Clinic, I shadowed two dentists and a hygienist. I watched a range of treatments including fillings, a root canal, extractions and orthodontic treatment. I found particularly interesting the fact that, although both dentists had very different personalities, they both related well to the patients, who seemed to find them very reassuring. A number of things surprised me; in particular, how demanding a dentist's day is.'*

It will be far easier to write this section of your personal statement if you kept notes in a reflective journal during your work experience as discussed in Chapter 2. Look back over what you wrote and use your thoughts and experiences as a stimulus for this section. With luck, the selectors may pick up on these experiences at interview and ask you to expand on some of your comments.

Following this, you should discuss the experiences you have had while undertaking any voluntary work. Any type of voluntary placement is a useful addition to your statement, but ongoing work in a care-based or clinical setting really boosts your profile. Opportunities often exist in care homes, children's hospices and hospitals and it is worth trying to contribute regularly over a long period of time rather than carrying it out for just a week or two. This type of experience can help you get an insight into patient care and the communication side of the profession and gives a really good opportunity to discuss how your interpersonal skills have developed while working with people. As with any dental work experience, you should make a note of any key experiences that you have had and what they have taught you, as this can then be commented on in your personal statement

Your academic interests

It is important for your personal statement to contain information about your academic interests and how they have furthered your desire to study dentistry. This may be related to some topics or practical skills that have been of particular interest to you over the course of your A level studies, or to an interesting article you have read in a newspaper or journal, or to something engaging you heard in a lecture. Whatever it is, it will help to demonstrate your desire to pursue the course, as long as you make it relevant to dentistry and put in sufficient detail. In so many personal statements this section struggles to get beyond 'I enjoyed learning about the human body' and 'I enjoy using different apparatus in practical work'; however, this is too generic to be meaningful. Keeping a journal over a long period of time of any wider reading that is relevant to dentistry will help this section to genuinely reflect what your interests are rather than being based on what you have panic read the week before submitting your application.

Evidence of developing skills and personal qualities

The person reading your UCAS application has to decide two things: whether you have the right skills and personal qualities to become a successful dentist, and whether you will be able to cope with and contribute to dental school life. To be a successful dentist, you need (among other things!) to:

- successfully pass your undergraduate studies
- have good interpersonal skills and get on with a wide range of people
- be able to work under pressure and cope with stress
- have well-developed manual skills.

How, then, does the person reading your personal statement know whether you have the qualities they are looking for? What you must remember is that the admissions tutor doesn't know you, so you have to give lots of evidence of how you have demonstrated and developed these qualities. Some of the things they may be looking for are:

- skill development during work experience/voluntary work
- positions of responsibility
- work in the local community
- an ability to get on with people
- participation in activities involving manual dexterity
- participation in team events
- involvement in school plays or concerts.

What they don't want to hear is how you have demonstrated interpersonal skills by going out with your friends every weekend or how you have improved your manual dexterity by playing PlayStation 4 games!

The selectors will be aware that some schools offer more to their students in the way of activities and responsibilities than others. However, even if there are very few opportunities made available to you through your school, you must still find ways to gain experience and develop your skills. You don't have to have been captain of the rugby team or gone on a three-month expedition to Borneo to be considered, but you do need to be able to demonstrate that you have made efforts to participate in a range of worthwhile activities.

Remember, however, that while evidence of all these skills and extra interests is extremely important, it will not compensate for lower grades, so having a strong academic profile and getting high grades still remain the most important aspects of your application.

Weak and strong personal statements: exemplars

The box below gives an example of a personal statement I have constructed based on experience of reading through what students write. It is made up of a combination of some good ideas, points that need to be expanded on, and things not to say! Overall, as you will probably notice, this would be considered a weak statement and would be unlikely to lead to an offer being made.

DO NOT COPY ANY PARTS OF THESE PERSONAL STATEMENTS!

You should use these examples to give you an idea of structure and the type of content you may want to include, but universities have sophisticated software to detect copied parts of personal statements so do not be tempted! Your personal statement should be personal to you, and, above all else, it should be honest.

Personal statement: Example 1 (character count: 1,859)

The role of a dentist is to look after the oral health of the patient and perform procedures such as root canals and fillings.

I first wanted to study medicine, but after discussing with my friend, I realised that dentistry was a much easier subject and would give me a chance to earn far more money. I have always liked science and so I think that dentistry would suit me perfectly. I really like the idea of giving people a perfect smile as I believe that a smile is a light in the window of the soul.

In my work experience I mainly watched the dentist see patients and observed procedures such as: fillings, root canals, scale and polish, denture fitting, tooth extraction and fitting of crowns and bridges. My voluntary work was really good and showed me how to work with people.

During my A levels, I have enjoyed studying my subjects. In chemistry, I have been really good at practical work and in biology, I really enjoy looking at the human body. I have not really enjoyed studying maths, but I have loved learning about modern European history and the events in the aftermath of the First World War that directly contributed to Hitler coming to power and the Second World War. I have found it fascinating how the political superpowers of the USA and USSR emerged from the aftermath of the war.

I also have a number of interests outside of school. I like relaxing and enjoy watching TV. I also like going out with my mates at the

---

weekend. I play football in a local league, read science fiction books, play the piano, go to the gym and listen to music. I also have a Saturday job which gives me some extra money to spend when I go out with my mates. An exclusive ubiquity of mine is that I am contented with mixing my social with my educational life at length, making the two important factors in my life none the less unabridged.

Personal statement: Example 1 raises a number of interesting points.

1. **It is too short.**

   This statement is just under 1,900 characters. The limit is 4,000 characters (including spaces) and you should aim to use as much of this as possible. Anything significantly below the character count will make a negative impression on the admissions tutors.

2. **It lacks detail and specific examples and has no reflection.**

   The candidate has got the right idea about the structure and attempted the key sections. However, it is very light on actual detail and doesn't really expand on any of the points made or give specific examples. When discussing work experience, go into detail about what you witnessed and reflect on what you learned. When giving details of what you are studying, be specific about topics you have enjoyed. This will give the admissions tutor a much greater insight into who you are and the skills you possess.

3. **It is not very personal.**

   This could be about any number of candidates applying to dentistry. Make sure your personal statement has evidence and experiences to show an admissions tutor who you really are and what you are genuinely interested in.

4. **It has a negative tone in relation to dentistry.**

   Unfortunately, many personal statements contain negative points about things that an applicant hasn't enjoyed studying or things they might not like about the career. These are sometimes included due to a misguided need to be brutally honest, but this really is not necessary. The overall tone should be optimistic and positive throughout.

5. **It wastes time telling them about dentistry.**

   Statements can often waste time by listing facts about dentistry or what dentists do. Remember that the people reading your statement will know all of this. Use the space instead to illustrate from your own experiences that you possess the qualities and skills that dentists need.

6. **It mentions money and potential earnings.**

   Although most dentistry applicants will have thought about how much money they will be making at some point, it is not something that needs to be highlighted in your personal statement. Your reasons for studying dentistry need to run much deeper than this if you are going to get into dental school.

7. **It seems too focused on cosmetic dentistry.**

   Lots of people fixate on the idea of specialising in cosmetic dentistry. However, dentistry is a far broader discipline and a personal statement should really reflect an understanding of this fact.

8. **It employs overused, repeated stock phrases.**

   Similes such as the smile being a window to the soul are cliched and can make an admissions tutor question whether your statement is an accurate picture of who you are. If you genuinely want to express an idea like this, think of how you could expand on it in your own words to make it more meaningful.

9. **It uses the vague idea of practical work to demonstrate manual dexterity.**

   If you are going to use the example of science practicals to demonstrate your manual dexterity, give specific examples of those you have enjoyed or apparatus you have used. You must also try to think of other activities that have helped you demonstrate these skills outside of your A level curriculum.

10. **It is very itemised.**

    It can be very easy to simply reduce your work experience and extracurricular activities to a long list. Take time to explain what you gained from each of your placements or interests and how they benefit your application. In addition to this, avoid mentioning mundane interests such as going out with friends and watching TV, because they tell the admissions tutor very little about you.

11. **It demonstrates the most passion when discussing an unrelated subject.**

    The only place in this statement that really comes close to the level of detail required is when it discusses A level History. Although it is great that this section uses lots of detail, the space would be better used discussing something more closely related to dentistry.

12. **It swallows a dictionary/thesaurus at the end.**

    Beware of overusing a dictionary or thesaurus. Obviously, you want your English to be as good as possible, but make sure that what you have written makes sense and sounds like you.

Although this statement is poor, it would not need much effort to make it a reasonable attempt, as the basic structure is fine. Your first attempt at writing a personal statement will probably be difficult and might not produce great results; however, it is important that you get feedback on your efforts and then redraft the statement as many times as necessary. The best personal statements can take up to 10 drafts to get completely right! Some suggestions for changes that would be worth making are shown in the following box.

The role of the dentist is to look after the oral health of the patient and perform procedures such as root canals and fillings. [*Develop this. It is a waste of time regurgitating what an admissions tutor will already know about dentistry as a career, so instead talk about why helping patients to look after their oral health interests you.*]

I first wanted to study medicine, but after discussing with my friend, I realised that dentistry was a much easier subject and would give me a chance to earn far more money. [*Do not mention other careers you have thought about. Focus on the one you are applying for.*] I have always liked science and so I think that dentistry would suit me perfectly. [*Expand on this to give much more detail about your reasons for wanting to pursue dentistry.*] I really like the idea of giving people a perfect smile as I believe that a smile is a light in the window of the soul. [*This is a real cliché, so think about what you want to say and put it into your own words to make it clear.*]

In my work experience I mainly watched the dentist see patients and observed procedures such as: fillings, root canals, scale and polish, denture fitting, tooth extraction and fitting of crowns and bridges. [*This lacks any real details about what your observations were and what it made you think about the profession. Make sure that any description is followed by careful reflection. What did you see that was of particular interest to you? What shocked you?*] My voluntary work was really good and showed me how to work with people. [*Give details. What did you do? When did you do it? How long was it for?*]

During my A levels, I have enjoyed studying my subjects. In chemistry, I have been really good at practical work and in biology, I really enjoy looking at the human body. [*Give specific detail. Which areas of biology and chemistry did you enjoy and why? Which practicals did you enjoy carrying out?*] I have not really enjoyed studying maths ... [*Don't put anything negative.*] ... but I have loved learning about modern European history and the events of the First World War that directly contributed to Hitler coming to power and the Second World War. In particular, I have found it fascinating how the political superpowers of the USA and USSR emerged from the aftermath of the war. [*This detail is great, but the characters need to be used to expand on areas that are more directly related to dentistry.*]

I also have a number of interests outside of school. I like relaxing and enjoy watching TV. I also like going out with my mates at the weekend. I play football in a local league, read science fiction books, play the piano, go to the gym and listen to music. I also have a Saturday job which gives me some extra money to spend when I go out with my mates. [*Ordinary interests are fine, but don't spend too much time discussing them. If you do want to put these things in, try to link to key skills that you have developed by doing them.*] An exclusive ubiquity of mine is that I am contented with mixing my social with my educational life at length making the two important factors in my life none the less unabridged. [*This is a typical thesaurus overload sentence that makes no sense. This can also come about from copying from other personal statements on the internet.*]

Here are two examples of much better personal statements based on those written by two students who both secured entry onto dental courses. Each demonstrates clarity and focus, and what comes through is the enthusiasm that the candidates have for dentistry.

Personal statement: Example 2 (character count: 3,835)

I first became interested in a career in dentistry after watching the transformation of a friend's mouth following multiple implants and orthodontic reconstruction. I was particularly attracted to how the practitioner was involved in all stages of treatment from diagnosis to resolution. Following this experience, further research and discussions with dentists illustrated that dentistry is going through a renaissance; a once feared system of tooth removal is being transformed into a technological art form that aims to keep teeth healthy and intact through life. My voluntary care-home placement also made me realise that the elderly are currently the most neglected group in terms of dental health. This has inspired me to want to play a role in helping this group of people to have well-preserved teeth.

During a week-long work placement at the Royal Stoke Hospital's Orthodontic and Restorative Unit, I witnessed major prosthetic reconstructive surgery on a female cancer patient. This involved tissue transplantation from the arm to the roof of the mouth; it had limited effect on the patient's physical appearance, yet markedly improved her emotional well-being. This experience confirmed my interest in the provision of psychological support and confidence to patients. I also prepared a wax nose prosthesis and learnt how to bend wire to make an 'Adam's Crib' appliance, which displayed to me the patience and manual dexterity required in such work. The additional three weeks spent in general and community dental surgeries allowed me to understand the time, emotional and financial pressures involved in such a career. I was also shown how scanning followed by 3D printing enables the preparation of perfectly fitting and long lasting ceramic prostheses within the surgery. I am excited about the benefits and opportunities created by such amazing technology, but also realise the need to balance the overall cost to the NHS.

Volunteering weekly for five months at a care home involved helping at meal times and providing activities for the residents. This strengthened my interpersonal skills and allowed me to see how the nursing staff dealt with the difficult situations. It also increased my knowledge of geriatric conditions and indicated the importance of mobile dental clinics. Similarly, I gained satisfaction from mentoring a 14-year-old mathematics student at my school; after one term of tutoring her exam score improved from 17% to 90%. These experiences involved careful listening to problems and encouraging progress.

During my A levels, I have had a particular interest in genetics. This led me to research the genetics underlying tooth development across species. At present such molecular studies are limited to specific and highly conserved dental genes in certain fish species, but they hold the key to future gene mapping across species. I am excited about how such research is expanding rapidly and will eventually revolutionise our understanding of both tooth development and decay. I have also found mathematics very intriguing and satisfying. At times it can be very frustrating, but that makes finding the solution all the more rewarding. I think I am naturally curious and find this to be a benefit in my academic studies.

Positions of responsibility, such as school prefect and hockey/house captain have enhanced my team building and time management skills. During the summer of 2015 I improved my spoken French by independently organising an exchange visit with a French student. I am an experienced musician – grade 8 in piano and grade 6 in trumpet. My commitment to the school orchestra, choir and jazz band has enhanced my teamwork skills while giving me the enjoyment of dealing with people. Musicianship has required application and has enhanced my dexterity. I am looking forward to utilising these attributes alongside the problem solving and continual learning in a challenging but rewarding career in dentistry.

Personal statement: Example 2 gives a real impression of dedication to pursuing dentistry and demonstrates a very clear and believable explanation of why this student wants to pursue dentistry. They have lots of relevant work experience and really make the most of expanding on what they have learned from it. In addition, this student has picked out key extracurricular activities and has elaborated on their importance. In particular, it strongly expresses an interest in orthodontics, but in a way that does not resort to clichés or mention the financially lucrative elements of this area.

Personal statement: Example 3 (character count: 3,764)

It was my work experience that cemented my desire to pursue dentistry. Here, I learnt that a dentist must not only develop scientific knowledge and practical skills, but must also be aware of their responsibility to serve the community. I felt that this was demonstrated when I observed an upset elderly patient inform the dentist of her husband's recent death. The care the dentist showed towards his patient was heart-warming and I realised that as a dentist you are able to help both medically and emotionally. I recognised the importance of sensitivity and building of trust to ensure a strong rapport. It was in this moment that I realised dentistry was the career for me.

I have spent six weeks shadowing dentists at work in NHS and private practices. I observed a wide range of procedures including root canals, fissure sealants and extractions. I found extractions fascinating as I loved being able to analyse and compare the roots of various teeth before their disposal. Whilst placing a filling on an anxious child I admired the dentist's ability to be focused and efficient as well as adopting an empathetic approach. The dentist explained each step of the procedure and reassured the child that they could interrupt treatment at any time by simply raising their hand. The significance of preventative care was reinforced as the dentist advised children with poor oral health on brushing techniques and quality of diet. Consequently the once anxious child left the practice not only physically healthier but with a new found confidence having overcome his fear. I found this immensely rewarding and it has drawn me towards paediatric dentistry as a future career option.

I thoroughly enjoyed my year of voluntary work at Victoria School for children with physical and cognitive disabilities where I helped entertain and feed the children on Friday afternoons. This taught me invaluable communication skills when dealing with learning impaired children and how to support them within school. Two months ago I started working at Explore Learning where I tutor and supervise children. Here I have been able to practise multitasking and have learnt the importance of patience when explaining to a child. For the past five years I have been an active member of a Ladies Guild at my place of worship. We prepare and serve food,

---

Getting into Dental School

assisting the young and the elderly. This has developed my ability to converse with all ages and religions and has strengthened my understanding of the wider community.

My interest in dentistry was fuelled further at a materials science course at Oxford University where I learnt about innovative aniso-tropic self-expanding tissue expanders which could potentially be used to repair cleft palate and crossbite. As part of my physics AS coursework I chose to research silver amalgam. I analysed amalgam's micro and macromolecular structure and how these proper-ties make it suitable for use in dental fillings.

I am working towards my Duke of Edinburgh Gold Award. Through determination, team effort and a good sense of humour we completed the expedition. For seven years, I was a member of the school hockey team and have been team captain, which involved leading and motivating a team, as well as delegating responsibility. At school I was a member of the Debating Society and was chosen to represent my school at the Oxford Schools' debating competition. In my spare time I enjoy fencing, playing the saxophone, embroidery and repairing small electronic items.

For me dentistry is the perfect combination of complex theory with practical association. I believe my hard work ethic, empathetic nature and dedication to professional development will prepare me for the challenges posed by such a demanding and fulfilling career.

Personal statement: Example 3 has a number of very strong elements. The point of a personal statement is that it should be personal and reflect as much as possible a candidate's individuality; I feel that this statement does this well. The depth of work experience that the candidate has also comes across and helps to show the admissions team that they have really spent time researching the demands of the profession. I certainly get the feeling that this student is genuinely interested in pursuing this career path for the right reasons.

Final points to remember before submitting your personal statement

- Your personal statement will require careful proofreading to ensure that your spelling, punctuation and grammar are sound and that there are no careless errors that have crept in. Beware of solely relying on computer software or internet based applications to do the checking for you; they will often misinterpret some of your phrases and perpetuate errors.

- It is worth getting another person to check your statement before submission. If you have been through it many times, it is unlikely you will spot errors that might be glaringly obvious to somebody else. However, beware of getting too many people to work on it as you can often end up with so many opinions that it can be hard to incorporate all of the ideas.
- Keep a copy of your statement so that you can use it as a reminder of what you have written. Remember that it is possible that an interviewer could use your personal statement as a starting point for a question, so you must be aware of what you said.
- Make sure that you are able to talk about all of the individual elements of your application at interview if needed. If there is anything you have included that you would not be able to discuss, remove it before submission.

University of Bristol

'Given the very large number of applications we receive each year from applicants who have achieved or are predicted to achieve high grades, we necessarily place substantial emphasis upon the quality of the personal statement. We look for:

- Motivation and commitment to dentistry
- Amount and variety of dental work experience, paid or unpaid (where possible this should be within various fields of dentistry)
- Evidence of manual dexterity (for example, playing an instrument, car or bike maintenance, art and craft activities)
- Evidence of teamwork and leadership
- Evidence of voluntary, charitable and/or mentoring activities
- Extracurricular interests, including sporting, musical and other personal achievements.'

Source: www.bristol.ac.uk/study/media/undergraduate/admissions-statements/2019/dentistry.pdf
Reprinted with kind permission of the University of Bristol

Queen's University Belfast

'Personal statements are not scored as part of the selection process and the following general factors are taken into account when considering applications:- (i) candidates are expected to state explicitly that Dentistry is their career choice. (Please note that an applicant cannot normally be considered for both Medicine and Dentistry.) There should be evidence of commitment and motivation in the personal statement. This should include evidence of what the candidate has done to find out about Dentistry as a career. Participation in

> activities within or outside School demonstrating transferable skills such as leadership, empathy, teamwork and communication skills are also considered.'
>
> Source: www.med.qub.ac.uk/docs/AdmissionPolicyDentistry-2019.pdf.
> Reprinted with kind permission of Queen's University Belfast.

Application checklist

- Do you have at least two weeks' dental-based work experience?
- Do you have evidence of ongoing voluntary work?
- Do you meet the GCSE entrance requirements for your chosen universities?
- Are you studying the correct combination of A level subjects?
- Are you on target for at least AAA?
- Have you researched the different dental schools and their courses?
- Have you been to university open days?
- Have you registered for/completed the UCAT and/or BMAT?
- Does your personal statement demonstrate the commitment, skills and attributes that the university is looking for?

What happens next?

- Immediately after UCAS receives your application, you will receive an email confirming receipt of your application. It is vital that you check this information carefully and inform UCAS if there are any inaccuracies. A common mistake is to select the foundation year – the 'pre-dental' year – rather than the start of the course proper, so make sure you haven't done this. Remember, you will be able to access your application at all times through the UCAS Track system using the same personal ID, username and password that you used to apply.
- As soon as UCAS processes your application, your prospective universities can access it, but they will be unable to see the other courses and universities that you have applied to, as long as they are not at the same institution. Once a university has accessed your application, it may contact you to acknowledge your application; however, not all universities bother doing this, so don't worry if you don't hear from them initially.
- The next stage is to wait to hear from the universities you applied to. If the universities feel that you have met their criteria, you will be invited to attend an interview. Some dental schools interview on a

first-come, first-served basis, while others wait until all applications are in before deciding whom to interview. It is not uncommon for students to hear nothing until after Christmas, so don't panic if you aren't contacted straight away.

- If your application is unsuccessful, you will receive a notification from UCAS telling you that you have been rejected by one or more of the dental schools. If this happens, don't despair: you may hear better news from another of the schools that you applied to. If you ultimately end up with four rejections, you should take the opportunity to carefully reassess whether dentistry is a realistic career ambition for you and whether there were any parts of your application that let you down. If you still feel that dentistry is for you, take the opportunity to strengthen any aspects of your application that were weak, for example undertaking further work experience. Under no circumstances should you give up and decide that it is no longer worth working hard in your academic studies; this will only reduce your chances of making a successful application the following year.
- Note that going through Clearing is not an option that you should bank on for entry into dentistry. Places are limited and often over-subscribed, and more offers are made than there are places. There can be the odd exception on a year-to-year basis where a few places are available through Clearing (although these are not usually advertised on Clearing lists); however, under no circumstances should you rely on any such places becoming available.

6| What makes a successful interview?

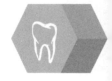

Once you've submitted your UCAS application, you must wait to hear from each of the universities you have applied to. If you meet their entry criteria and they feel that your application is strong in the areas they deem to be most important, they may call you for interview. The universities use interviews to find out first hand whether the picture painted by your application is accurate and to investigate whether you have the skills necessary to succeed on the course.

In this section, we will consider both multiple mini and panel types of interview and the specific steps you will need to go through in order to prepare yourself, as well as more general interview pointers. Most of this guidance will be relevant to both types of interview and give appropriate general interview advice, but differences will be highlighted where necessary.

Multiple mini interviews

In the past, the vast majority of dental interviews have been panel-based, where two or more interviewers ask applicants a series of questions in a similar fashion to a traditional job interview. However, in recent years, a significant number of universities have moved towards the system of multiple mini interviews (MMIs), although a small number still retain the panel style of interview.

The MMI is designed to judge the suitability of a candidate to study dentistry, and is felt to give a more accurate indication of future academic performance during the course. This style of interview will have some similarities with the panel interview; however, the major difference is that applicants participate in a number of small interviews and tasks rather than just sitting in one place answering questions for the whole interview. For example, the MMI at Leeds consists of eight six-minute mini interviews, with interviewees having a minute in-between stations. The format of each station will vary, but you will receive instructions explaining what you will be required to do, so ensure that you listen carefully and read any written instructions to give you a good idea of what you will be facing.

There are two main reasons for dental schools using this type of interview. Firstly, research has suggested that traditional panel interviews give a poor indication of the likely performance of the interviewee as an undergraduate; the MMI improves on this. Secondly, one of the major criticisms of the panel interview is that students can be heavily coached on the vast majority of question types and, as a result, do not give an accurate indication of their personality and character attributes at interview. MMIs are therefore specifically designed to test those attributes of the interviewee that are unlikely to be improved by participating in preparation courses. They thereby allow the dental school to build a truer picture of what each candidate is like.

Some universities are relatively tight-lipped about the exact detail of the MMI and give little information to the interviewees, while others are more open to sharing the details of exactly what will be faced.

Queen's University Belfast gives detailed exemplar material and short tutorial video clips illustrating what will be faced at each station (visit www.qub.ac.uk/schools/mdbs/Study/Medicine/HowtoApply/MMIs), whereas Bristol gives a brief paragraph outlining the basic setup:

University of Bristol

'Applicants are assessed using an evidence-based Multiple Mini Interview (MMI) system, covering different aspects of the skills and knowledge required to be a successful dental student and dentist.'

Source: www.bristol.ac.uk/study/media/undergraduate/
admissions-statements/2019/dentistry.pdf
Reprinted with kind permission from the University of Bristol
Please note that this information is relevant to the current admissions cycle. The information is reviewed each year, and may be different for the next admissions cycle, so make sure to check the university website for the most up-to-date information.

Below are some sample MMI questions provided by www.multiplemini interview.com.

Station #1

PROMPT (Read and consider for 2 minutes):

Joe is a pizza delivery worker. The pizza shop he works for has a 30 minutes or less delivery guarantee or else the customer does not have to pay. On Joe's most recent delivery, he spots a woman bleeding on the street. There is no one else around and the woman seems to be unable to move by herself. However, Joe knows that if he returns empty handed again, he will be fired from this job which he most desperately needs. What do you think Joe should do? Justify your solution in terms of practical and ethical considerations.

YOUR RESPONSE: (Speak for 8 minutes)

Station #2

PROMPT (Read and consider for 2 minutes):

Discuss one of your pastimes outside of school and how the skills you acquired help you in your career.

YOUR RESPONSE: (Speak for 8 minutes)

Station #3:

PROMPT (Read and consider for 2 minutes):

Clostridium difficile (C. difficile) is a type of bacteria that increases its activity with most antibiotic use, and is therefore very difficult to treat. Research shows that the most effective way to prevent the spread of infection is frequent handwashing. However, many people have flat-out refused to wash their hands in hospitals. The government is contemplating passing a policy to make it mandatory for people entering hospitals to wash their hands or else risk being taken out of the building against their will. Do you think the government should go ahead with this plan? Consider and discuss the legal, ethical or practical problems that exist for each action option and conclude with a persuasive argument supporting your decision.

YOUR RESPONSE: (Speak for 8 minutes)

Source: www.multipleminiinterview.com
Reproduced with kind permission by Astroff Consultants Inc., St. Clair Avenue East, Suite 800, Toronto, Ontario, Canada M4T 2T5 at www.astroffconsultants.com

Based on these few questions, it is clear that is are a broader range of skills that need to be prepared for an MMI compared with a panel interview. Although an MMI is less formulaic than a panel interview, candidates can still take a number of steps to ensure that they are as prepared as possible, even if they might not be fully aware of what to expect until the day of the interview itself. Students should consider the following points in advance of their interview as they are the basis for the vast majority of questions.

- Communication is one of the key skills that will be assessed in the MMI, so you should therefore work on developing your ability to communicate information clearly. There are numerous ways of testing this, such as:
  - asking you to explain your interest in dentistry or your reasons for applying to the university
  - asking you to describe a picture or a painting
  - asking you to describe a series of instructions to carry out a basic task.

  In reality, any station where you are going to be speaking will be directly or indirectly assessing your ability to communicate.

Example: You are given a picture of *Sunflowers* by Van Gogh and are asked to describe it in as much detail as possible by the interviewer.

- Communicating with different groups of people is a vital skill that dentists need. You should therefore reflect on how you might communicate effectively with different groups of people, for example children, the elderly, or individuals with disabilities. Many MMIs include role play exercises to test how effectively you can interact with people in a variety of situations. It is therefore important to be able to put into practice your thoughts on how you would communicate with different people.

Example: You are asked to explain what factors you might need to consider when explaining a treatment plan to a patient with autism.

Example: You are given the following scenario: You are working in a café and a customer comes to you with a complaint about the quality of her food. You need to deal with this customer and resolve her complaint.

- Practise basic manual dexterity tasks, as a number of MMIs have a section where candidates will be expected to complete some form of manual exercise. Try carrying out tasks that require repetition, focus and a steady hand as these are what the tasks are likely to be based on. To prepare for this, practise following instructions to make origami shapes, or bend wire with pliers to make shapes or patterns.

Example: You are given a step-by-step guide to making an origami frog. You must follow the instructions to try and complete the task within three minutes.

- Practise basic observation and memory tasks. If you are shown an object for 30 seconds, can you accurately recall what it is like when it is taken away from you? If you are shown a range of objects all at once, how many can you recall a minute later?

Example: You are given a tray of 10 objects. You must try to remember what the objects are and key details about them. When the objects are removed, you must answer questions about the things you have just seen.

- Consider your motivation for studying the course. This may be asked directly, but even if it is not, then having a clear idea of your motivation will help to guide your answers to other questions.

Example: You are asked to explain what appeals to you about becoming a dentist.

- Make sure you understand what the key features of the university are and how the course is delivered. You may be required to explain why you are interested in studying at the university and it is this knowledge that will help you to formulate an answer.

Example: You are asked to explain your reasons for applying to the university.

- Revisit your personal statement and reflect on key experiences in terms of work experience, leadership, teamwork, motivation, etc. You should be prepared to give evidence of how you have demonstrated that you have the skills necessary to be a dentist. Start by listing the key attributes that you think a dentist needs to master and then list at least one piece of evidence from your experiences that demonstrates you have each skill or have developed it.

Example: You are asked to explain what is meant by empathy and then asked to share an experience where you have had to demonstrate this attribute.

- Look at different methods of data presentation, for example, different styles of table and graph. Practise describing to somebody what is being shown by these graphical representations.

Example: Describe the main trends shown by this graph. Can you suggest reasons for the patterns shown.

Figure 2 Percentage of 5-year-old children with decay experience in England, 2012

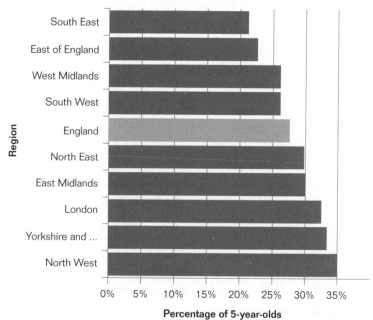

Source: www.england.nhs.uk/wp-content/uploads/2014/02/
dental-info-pack.pdf

- Some interviews require students to give a presentation to the interviewer, so it is vital to practise your presentation skills and your ability to deliver information to an audience.

  Example: You are asked in advance to produce a one-minute presentation about a hobby that you are passionate about and are then asked questions about this by the interviewer.

- Practise responding to situations involving ethical dilemmas in both clinical and non-clinical contexts. An understanding of the standards required of dental professionals can help you to respond appropriately to such situations. These can be found at https://standards.gdc-uk.org.

  Example: While treating a patient, they ask for all of their teeth to be removed and replaced with dental implants. How do you respond to this situation and what ethical issues does it raise?

  Often, interview questions can incorporate completely random elements that seem unrelated to the dental profession. These are usually designed to see what your communication skills are like and if you can stay calm in unexpectedly stressful situations.

  Example: You are asked to describe your family.

- Read the invitation to interview letter that the university has sent to you. Often this will give you more details about what to expect on the day and may drop some subtle hints about the interview process.

- Consider and practise the questions that are likely to be asked at a panel interview (see below). Although most of them probably won't come up in the MMI, they will still provide you with opportunities to hone your communication skills and reflect on your experience and motivation. This will help to improve the overall impression you make.

Panel interviews

As discussed above, the traditional panel-style interview is being phased out by a number of dental schools to be replaced by the MMI. Although this type of interview is somewhat easier to prepare for due to the well-known nature of the potential questions, it can be very easy to fall into the trap of memorising pre-rehearsed answers. The questions that are listed on pages 87–93 are designed to give you an opportunity to gather your thoughts and reflect on the various aspects of your application rather than devise set answers that you then rehearse and regurgitate in an interview.

Table 5 Typical interviews – 2018/19

University	Type of interview	Number on panel	Other information
Belfast	MMIs designed to test a range of non-cognitive skills	Each mini interview is conducted by a pair of interviewers	Scores at interview are used to rank applicants. Offers are made to the highest-ranking interviewees
Birmingham	MMIs	n/a	Circuit of 10–12 stations, approximately 1 hour in total
Bristol	MMIs	n/a	Score will be ranked and offers made to those with the highest scores
Cardiff	MMIs	n/a	12 stations in total, each station 5 minutes maximum, 2 stations are rest stations
Dundee	MMIs	n/a	Consists of 10 7-minute interviews
Glasgow	MMIs	n/a	None
King's	MMIs	n/a	40–50 minutes in total
Leeds	MMIs	n/a	MMI lasts for about 2 hours
Liverpool	MMIs	n/a	None
Manchester	MMIs	n/a	7 stations, each 7 minutes long; 2-minute gap between stations to prepare for the next one
Newcastle	Panel interview	2	The interview lasts for approximately 20 minutes
Plymouth	MMIs	n/a	7 stations, the interview lasts for approximately 50 minutes
Queen Mary	Panel interview	3	The panel can include tutors, admissions staff, dentists and current students
Sheffield	Panel interview	3	The panel comprises 2 members of academic staff and a senior dental student. The interview lasts for up to 15 minutes

Questions for you to reflect on in preparation for your interview (MMI and Panel)

The questions discussed below should be considered regardless of the type of interview that you are attending. Although you will not be asked the majority of these questions in an MMI, preparing responses will help you to develop a real understanding of your reasons for applying and this will shine through in subtle ways in any interview.

Question: Why did you decide to apply to this dental school?

Comment: The panel will be looking for evidence of research, and that your reasons are based on informed judgement rather than just picking a university randomly from a list. Probably the best possible answer would start with 'I came to your open day …', because you can then proceed to tell them why you like their university so much, what impressed you about the university and facilities, and how the atmosphere of the place would particularly suit you. If you are/were unable to attend open days, try to arrange a formal or informal visit before you are interviewed so that you can show you are aware of the environment, both academic and physical, and that you like the place. If you know people who are at the dental school or university, so much the better.

You should also know about the course structure; the website will give detailed information. Although on the surface all dental courses appear to cover broadly the same subjects, there are big differences between the ways in which courses are delivered and in the opportunities for patient contact, and your interviewers will expect you to know about their specific course.

Another useful source of information is the Unistats website (https://unistats.direct.gov.uk), which gives details of student feedback about each university and each course they offer. If there are particular areas that a university scores very highly on, it may be worth mentioning as a factor that has influenced your decision.

Answers to avoid are, for example, ones such as 'Reputation' (unless you know in detail the areas for which the dental school is highly regarded), 'I don't want to move away from my friends', 'You take a lot of retake students' or 'My dad says it's easy to get a place here'.

Question: Why do you want to be a dentist?

Comment: This is the question that all interviewees expect. Given that the interviewers will be aware that you are expecting the question, they will also expect your answer to be carefully planned. If you look surprised and say something like 'Um … well … I haven't really thought about why …' you can expect to be rejected. Other answers to avoid are those along the lines of 'The money' or 'It's easier than medicine'.

Many students are worried that they will sound insincere when they answer this question. The way to avoid this is to try to bring in reasons that are personal to you: for instance, an incident that sparked your interest (perhaps a visit to your own dentist), or an aspect of your work experience that particularly fascinated you. The important thing is to try to express clearly what interested you instead of generalising your answers. Rather than saying 'Dentistry combines science, working with people and the chance to have control over your career' – which says little about you – tell the interviewers about the way in which your interest progressed.

Here is an example of a carefully considered answer.

> *'I used to really enjoy going to the dentist when I was young. My dentist was brilliant at explaining things clearly and patiently, and I was interested in the technology that was being used. When I was thinking about my career, I arranged to shadow another dentist, and the more time I spent at the surgery, the more I realised that I had the skills to follow this career. It also gave me the chance to find out about what being a dentist is really like. The things that particularly interest me about dentistry are ...'*

It is vital that you do not learn this quote and repeat it at your interview. Ensure that your answer is not only personal to you, but also honest. With luck, the interviewers will pick up on something that you said about work experience and ask you more questions about this. Since 'Why do you want to be a dentist?' is such an obvious question, interviewers often try to find out the information in different ways. Expect questions such as 'When did your interest in dentistry start?' or 'What was it about your work experience that finally convinced you that dentistry was for you?'

Question: I see that you spent two weeks with your dentist. Was there anything that surprised you?

Comment: Variations on this question could include 'Was there anything that particularly interested you?', 'Was there anything you found off-putting?' or simply 'Tell me about your work experience'. What these questions really mean is: 'Are you able to show us that you were interested in what was happening during your work experience?'

Returning to the original question, answering either 'Yes' or 'No' without explanation will not gain you many marks. Similarly, saying 'Yes, I was surprised by the number of patients who seemed very scared' says nothing about your awareness of the dentist's approach to their patients. However, answering: 'Yes, I was surprised by the number of patients who seemed very scared. What struck me, however, was the way in which the dentist dealt with each patient as an individual, sometimes being sympathetic, sometimes explaining things in great detail and sometimes using humour to relax them. For instance ...' shows that you were interested enough to be aware of more than the most obvious things.

Sentences that start with 'For example ...' and 'For instance ...' are particularly important, as they allow you to demonstrate your interest. As previously mentioned in chapter 2, you should keep a diary of things that you saw during your work experience so that you do not forget and can provide examples. You should then review your diary before interview to refresh your memory.

Question: Can you tell me about something that you have read recently in relation to dentistry?

Comment: If you are interested in making dentistry your career, the selectors will expect you to be interested enough in the subject to want to read about it. Some good sources of information that you may want to make use of are the GDC website (www.gdc-uk.org), www.dentistry. co.uk, the BBC news website and broadsheet newspapers. You should get into the habit of checking the news every day to see if there are any dentistry-related stories. You should not just rely on things that you read years ago; however, you may have followed a particular issue for a number of years, and it is totally appropriate in this situation to revisit historical items in order to give depth to something you have read more recently.

Question: During your work experience, you had the chance to discuss dentistry with the practitioner. What do you know about the way NHS dentists are paid?

Comment: You must be aware of the nuts and bolts of running a dental practice; in particular, it is worth understanding the difference between NHS and private work and the way in which the NHS is funded. You should also have an idea about what a dentist earns and what proportion of it goes back into running the practice. Similar questions might focus on how much dentists are paid for different types of treatment, or how much NHS patients pay for treatment.

Question: Should dental treatment be free on the NHS?

Comment: Although not specifically about dentistry, this type of question can be useful for an admissions tutor to see how you can think on your feet about wider issues. Obviously this type of question needs you to understand what the issues surrounding the NHS are and to have knowledge of what is going on in the world; but more importantly, it needs you to be able to form and express argumnets and opinions. If you are struggling to figure out exactly how to respond to such a question, it is worth taking a moment to gather your thoughts before you reply. It is also worth considering both sides of the argument and expressing your reflection on these, as it shows that you have an appreciation of the range of issues involved.

Question: What qualities should a dentist possess?

Comment: Don't simply list the qualities. The interviewer hasn't asked the question because the interviewer is puzzled about what these qualities are; they have asked it to give you a chance to show that you are aware of them, and that you possess them. The best way to answer this is to use phrases such as 'During my work experience at the Smith and Smith Dental Practice, I was able to observe/talk to the dentist, and I became aware that …', or 'Communication is very important: for instance, when I was shadowing my dentist, there was a patient who …' Always try to relate these general questions to your own experiences.

Question: Do you know what periodontics is?

Comment: It is highly unlikely that you will be asked specific questions in relation to the technical aspects of dentistry as you haven't yet studied the subject. However, something you have written in your personal statement or mentioned in one of your responses might move the conversation in this direction. This provides another good reason for carrying out careful research into the field of dentistry before applying and for asking questions during work experience. Remember that when you are asked this type of question, the interviewer is not expecting you to have an encyclopaedic knowledge of the area, but is interested in seeing whether you have a solid basic knowledge. It would be worth starting your answer with a basic definition and then, if you have further knowledge or experience of the area, expanding on it. It may also provide another opportunity to discuss a relevant article or current issue that you have seen or to further discuss an experience from a work placement.

If you have absolutely no idea about what is being asked, try first to think about whether you have any reference points that might enable you to make an educated guess; in this situation it is preferable to discuss your ideas and to show the interviewers your thought processes than to just stay silent and refuse to answer. There are times when an interviewer will purposely ask a question that is difficult just so they can see how you respond under pressure and if you can think on your feet.

Questions about manual dexterity

Question: Dentistry requires a high degree of manual dexterity. How have you developed this skill?

Comment: The question about manual dexterity is very interesting and often ignored by candidates. Manual dexterity means being able to perform intricate tasks with your hands. Dentists have to work in a confined and sensitive area (the mouth) using precision instruments, in situations where accuracy is vital and where there is little margin for error. If you have trouble picking up a coffee cup without knocking it over or if you always press the wrong keys when you work on a computer, dentistry may not be the best career for you. The interviewers will need to be reassured that you have the manual skills to be able to work on other people's teeth. Good examples of tasks that require a high degree of manual dexterity include sewing, embroidery, model-making and playing a musical instrument.

Manual dexterity is a very important factor that should not be overlooked in the selection process. Students, professionals and admissions tutors to whom I've spoken have all indicated that without this quality a prospective candidate might as well not continue with his or her application. If you are not able to give an example of your own skills, take up a hobby that involves precision work, before it is too late. Admissions tutors don't want students bringing examples of their handiwork to interview, but you do need be able to discuss any relevant experiences.

Whatever you do, do not lie about the examples of manual dexterity that you provide. One admissions tutor tells the story of a young man who claimed that he liked icing cakes in his spare time. He brought in photographs of some of the cakes he had iced but it became clear, after very little questioning, that it was his mother who had actually done the work. This did not go down well with the panel, as you can imagine!

Questions to find out what sort of person you are

Question: How do you cope with stress?

Comment: Dentistry can be a stressful occupation. Dentists have to deal with difficult people, those who are scared and those who react badly when in a dental surgery. Furthermore, there are few 'standard' situations: everyone's mouth and teeth are different, as are their problems, and things can go wrong. In these circumstances, the dentist cannot panic but must remain calm and rational. In addition, the nature of the profession means that the financial aspects of running a business may also be a source of stress. The interviewers want to make a judgement as to whether you will be able to cope with the demands that the course and the job throw up. Once again, be sincere. Reflect on a particularly stressful time in your life and how you have coped through it. Remember, it is always best to use experiences from your own life than to talk generally.

Question: I see that you enjoy reading. What is the most recent book that you have read?

Comment: Although it may sound obvious, if you have written that you enjoy reading on your UCAS application, make sure that you have actually read something recently. Admissions tutors will be able to tell you stories about interviewees who look at them with absolute surprise when they are asked about books, despite reading featuring in the personal statement. Answers such as 'Well … I haven't had much time recently, but … let me see … I read *Top Gear* magazine last month, and … oh yes … I had to read *Jane Eyre* for my English GCSE' will not help your chances. The same advice is also true for any other interests you put on your personal statement: if you put it down, you need to be prepared to talk about it!

Question: What interests do you have?

Comment: Don't say 'Watch TV' or 'Go shopping'. Mention something that involves working or communicating with others, for instance sport or music. Use the question to demonstrate that you possess the qualities required in a dentist. However, don't make your answer so insincere that the interviewers realise that you are trying to impress them. Saying 'I relax most effectively when I go to the local dental surgery to shadow the dentist' will not convince them.

Other questions to consider

Remember that you will have only limited time in an interview and as a result will only be asked a relatively modest number of questions. There is therefore no chance of you being asked all of the questions listed below, but preparing as widely as possible will help to increase your all-round knowledge and skills, which will come across at any interview you attend.

- Why do you want to be a dentist?
- What have you done to investigate dentistry?
- Give me an example of how you cope with stress.
- Why did you apply to this dental school?
- During your work experience, did anything surprise you?
- During your work experience, did anything shock you?
- Tell me about preventive dentistry.
- If you had to organise a campaign to improve oral health, how would you go about it?
- What role do dentists play in improving oral health?
- Why do dentists recommend the fluoridation of water supplies?
- There has been a good deal of negative publicity about mercury fillings. Do you think that they are dangerous?
- What is gingivitis?
- How are NHS dentists funded?
- Have you read any articles about dentistry recently?
- What advances can we expect in dental technology/treatment in the future?
- What have you done to demonstrate your commitment to the community?
- What would you contribute to this dental school?
- What are your best/worst qualities?
- What was the last novel that you read? Did you like it?
- What do you do to relax?
- What is your favourite A level subject?
- Do dentists treat children differently from adults?

- What precautions need to be taken with patients who are HIV positive?
- What is the role of the dental nurse/technician?
- How does teamwork apply to the role of a dentist?
- What role does a dentist have in diagnosing other medical problems?

How to succeed in the interview

You should prepare for both types of interview as if you are preparing for an examination. Start by revisiting your personal statement as this can be a common starting point for interviewers when thinking about questions to ask you. In particular, revisit the details of your work experience so that you can recount details of your time with a dentist and reflect on the key experiences you had and lessons you learned. Then look through articles you have saved from the newspaper, the internet and magazines in relation to dentistry, and consider all the things that you have mentioned in your personal statement. It is vital that you are truthful in your personal statement, as it is very easy to get caught out if you have lied.

When you are preparing for an interview, try to have at least one mock interview so that you can get some feedback on your answers. Your school may be able to help you. If not, there are many providers that offer a mock interview service. Friends of your parents may also be able to help. As mentioned previously, do not memorise set answers to questions; this is very easy to spot during an interview and will make you seem insincere. It is much better to have a good idea of roughly what you want to say and then put it across in a natural way. If possible, video your mock interview so that you are aware of the way you come across in such a situation.

At the end of your interview

In a panel situation you may be given the opportunity to ask a question at the end, although this won't happen in an MMI. Bear in mind that the interviews are carefully timed, and that your attempts to impress the panel with 'clever' questions may do quite the opposite. The golden rule is: only ask a question if you are genuinely interested in the answer (which, of course, is one you were unable to find the answer to on the website or when speaking to other people during your visit). Remember that the people interviewing you have lots to do and very little time to do it in, so most questions are better off asked to staff or current students that you meet at other points on the day of your interview.

Questions to avoid

- What is the structure of the first year of the course?
- Will I be able to live in a hall of residence?
- When will I first have contact with patients?

As well as being boring questions, the answers to these will be available in the prospectus. If you need to ask these questions, it will be obvious to your interviewers that you have not done any serious research.

Remember: if in doubt, don't ask a question. End by saying: 'All of my questions have been answered by the prospectus and the students who showed me around the dental school. Thank you very much for an interesting day.' Smile, shake hands (if appropriate) and say goodbye.

General interview tips

As in any interview, appearance and body language are just as important as the answers you give to the questions you are being asked. The impression that you create can have a big impact. Remember that if the interviewers cannot picture you as a dentist in the future, they are unlikely to offer you a place.

Body language

- Make eye contact with the interviewers, but don't stare at them!
- When you say hello to the interviewer, remember to smile.
- Sit up straight, but adopt a position that you feel comfortable in.
- Don't wave your hands around too much, but don't keep them gripped together to stop them moving either. Fold them across your lap, or rest them on the arms of the chair.
- Avoid annoying and repetitive body movements, such as jiggling your leg or tapping the table.

Speech

- Talk at your normal pace and beware of speaking too quickly. When you are nervous it is very easy to speed up your speech, so make a conscious effort to slow down if needed.
- Don't use slang or offensive language.
- Avoid saying 'Erm ...', 'You know', 'Sort of' and 'Like'. These are often put into sentences without really realising; another good reason to have mock interviews so that these habits can be highlighted to you.
- Say 'Hello' at the start of the interview, and thank the interviewer(s) and say 'Goodbye' at the end.

Dress and appearance

- Wear clothes that show you have made an effort for the interview. In reality, this should mean formal, smart dress. If you are unsure, it is better to be overdressed than underdressed and have no way of making yourself look smarter.
- Make sure that you are clean and tidy.
- Avoid using overpowering perfume or aftershave.
- Clean your nails and shoes.
- Wash your hair.
- Avoid excessive piercings.

How you are selected

During the interview, the interviewers (both MMI and panel) will be assessing you in various categories. Each interviewer follows careful guidelines to mark your performance so that they can compare each candidate fairly.

The scoring system will vary from university to university, but you are likely to be scored in a number of categories, with the dental school setting a minimum mark that you will have to gain if you are to be made an offer. For example, Bristol University gives the following information about the scoring of its MMI interview.

University of Bristol

'Interviewees' performance on the MMIs will be scored by assessors and ranked by the admissions office. Those with the strongest overall performance will receive offers.'

Source: www.bristol.ac.uk/study/media/undergraduate/
admissions-statements/2019/dentistry.pdf
Reprinted with kind permission from the University of Bristol
Please note that this information is relevant to the current admissions cycle. The information is reviewed each year, and may be different for the next admissions cycle, so make sure to check the university website for the most up-to-date information.

If you are below the cut-off score but close to it, you may be put on an official or unofficial waiting list. If you are offered a place, you will receive a letter from the dental school telling you what you need to achieve in your A levels: this is called a conditional offer. In addition, the conditions of your offer will be added to UCAS Track, although this can take some time, so don't worry if you are made to wait a while. Post-A level students who have achieved the necessary grades will be given unconditional offers in terms of the academic requirements, but may still be made conditional offers in relation to criminal record and health checks.

If you are unlucky, all you will get is a notification from UCAS saying that you have been rejected. If this happens, it is not necessarily the end of the road in dentistry, as you may be able to reapply as a post-A level applicant. What you must do in this situation is contact the universities that you applied to and ask for feedback about why you were unsuccessful. Some universities will be more helpful than others and give relatively detailed feedback, which will give you points to consider. However, be warned, some universities don't give feedback, while others will just send a standard letter with no details about your particular application.

What happens next?

When UCAS has received replies from all of your choices you will then have about a month to make up your mind about where you want to go. If you have only one offer, you have two choices. One is to accept the choice and aim to get the grades to go to that university, happy in the knowledge that you are going to study the course of your dreams; the other is to reject the choice, if you have decided for whatever reason that you don't want to go to that university. If you choose to go down the latter route, you must then apply either the following year or add additional choices through what is known as UCAS Extra, although it is highly unlikely at this point in time that places for dentistry will appear on Extra.

If you have more than one offer, you have to accept one as your firm choice, and may accept another as your insurance choice. If the place where you really want to study makes a lower offer than one of your other choices, do not be tempted to choose the lower offer as your insurance choice since you are obliged to go to the dental school that you have put as your firm choice if you achieve the necessary grades. If you narrowly miss the grades required by your firm offer, you may still be accepted on the course. You would have to accept this offer so you would not be able to go to your insurance choice. You can go to your insurance choice only if your firm choice will not accept you. So, if you had put the dental school you really wanted to study at as your insurance choice, in this instance you would not be able to accept a place there.

If you are unsuccessful, there remains the option of completing a first degree and then attempting graduate entry or studying dentistry overseas (see page 121).

Current issues in dentistry

As part of your research into dentistry and during your work experience, you will probably come across news and other relevant articles about a range of current issues related to the profession. While an awareness of what is going on in the world of dentistry may not be of any use in choosing which dental school to apply to, it is absolutely essential when it comes to your preparation for interview, as you will be expected to have a solid understanding of such issues. The aim of this section, therefore, is to give you an idea of some of these issues and provide a starting point for you to do further research. While you are reading and researching, it is important once again to keep a notebook to hand so that you can jot down anything of interest; your notes will then be the perfect starting point for your revision when you receive notice of your first interview. There is a wealth of information relating to the world of dentistry, but, in my experience, sites like www.dentistry.co.uk, www.bda.org, www.dentalhealth.org and www.bbc.co.uk are worth checking frequently to keep abreast of important developments.

Sugar tax on soft drinks

In 2016, the government announced plans for a sugar tax to be introduced on soft drinks depending on the quantity of sugar in the drink. This tax came into force in April 2018 and is currently levied at the rate of 18p per litre on drinks with more than 5g of sugar per 100ml and 24p per litre on drinks with more than 8g per 100ml.

In the lead up to the implementation of the tax, many of the leading soft-drink manufacturers altered the recipes of the products that would be affected in order to lower sugar levels. Brands such as Fanta, Lucozade, Vimto and Ribena have already made significant and noticeable reductions. However, not all sugary drinks are included in the tax. Notable exceptions are pure fruit juices (as extra sugar isn't added) and drinks with a certain volume of milk (due to the benefits of calcium).

Table 6 Examples of drinks with reduced sugar content

Drink	Original sugar content (g per 100ml)	New sugar content (g per 100mlg)
Irn Bru	10.3	4.7
Lucozade	13	4.5
Ribena	10	Less than 4.5

When the idea was initially proposed, it was expected that it would raise approximately £500 million per year in tax receipts, however, due to the steps taken by manufacturers, this figure has been revised down to approximately £240 million. The supporters of the tax have used this information to point to the success that there has already been in driving down sugar content in drinks.

Similar types of tax across the globe have had some success in reducing consumption of fizzy drinks. For example, Mexico introduced a 10% sugar tax in 2014. Within the first year, there was a 12% reduction in fizzy drink sales. There is no doubt that this type of tax has the potential to have a massive effect on oral health, but only time will tell as to whether there is a significant impact in the UK.

The nation's oral health

There has been a steady improvement in oral health in the UK since 1978. According to data published by the NHS in 2014 (www.england. nhs.uk/wp-content/uploads/2014/02/dental-info-pack.pdf):

- approximately 25% of over 65s had lost all of their natural teeth in 2009, compared to nearly 80% in 1978
- over 60% of adults still had 21 or more natural teeth in 2009, compared to 30% in 1978.

Some of the reasons for the improvement are:

- fluoridation of water
- fluoride in toothpaste
- developments in dental treatment
- provision of preventive and restorative dental treatment
- increased awareness of dental health.

There has been a significant push by organisations such as the British Dental Health Foundation to raise public awareness of the need for good general oral health. This has been achieved by carrying out educational campaigns such as National Smile Month and providing information to the public regarding issues such as mouth cancer and fluoridation. It is important to recognise the shift from talking about good dental health to talking about good oral health: this represents the fact that it is the health not just of the teeth but of the whole mouth that is important. Promoting the virtues of good oral health in this way continues to have a significant impact on levels of public awareness.

The National Institute for Health and Clinical Excellence (NICE) has published guidelines on the frequency of dental check-ups. The recommended interval between check-ups has been the same (usually six months) regardless of the patient's age and oral health, but the official NHS guidance states:

> 'You may assume you should have a dental check-up every 6 months, but some people may not need to go so often and others may need more frequent checks. Your dentist will suggest when you should have your next check-up based on how good your oral health is. The time between check-ups can vary from 3 months to 2 years, depending on how healthy your teeth and gums are and your risk of future problems.'

Source: www.nhs.uk/live-well/healthy-body/dental-check-ups

Children's oral health

Every 10 years, an extensive national survey is conducted regarding the oral health of children. The 2013 survey results, published in 2015, revealed that although there was a reduction in the 'extent and severity' of tooth decay in the permanent teeth of 12–15-year-olds between 2003 and 2013, a large percentage of children continue to be affected by tooth decay. (Source: NHS Digital, https://digital.nhs.uk/data-and-information/areas-of-interest/public-health/children-s-dental-health-survey.)

Professor Liz Kay, Scientific Adviser to the BDA (quoted on the BDA's website), said:

> 'While this report does demonstrate a welcome overall improvement in children's dental health, the gulf between those with the best and worst oral health persists. This report shows that a high percentage of our children still suffer unacceptable levels of tooth decay.'

There is no doubt that concerns regarding the oral health of children stem from the high levels of sugar in their diet. One of the major contributing factors towards tooth decay and erosion in children is the consumption of fizzy drinks; children who drink several fizzy drinks a day massively increase the chance of damage occurring to their teeth.

A survey conducted in 2017 by Public Health England about the oral health of five-year-old children (https://assets.publishing.service.gov.uk/government/uploads/system/uploads/attachment_data/file/708157/NDEP_for_England_oral_health_survey_5yr_2017_report.pdf) revealed some interesting facts. The main finding was that only 76.7% of five-year-olds were free from obvious decay. In spite of the progress made with children's oral health in recent decades, this is still a shocking statistic. As a consequence, it is a certainty that improving the oral health of young children will continue to be a hot topic. There is also no doubt that the success of the sugar tax on improving these statistics will be scrutinised carefully in years to come.

Mouth cancer

What is mouth cancer?

Mouth cancer is historically thought of as a disease affecting mainly older males; however, over recent years, the incidence in women and children has significantly increased. One of the major issues with mouth cancer is that there is poor public awareness of the disease and its symptoms. Mouth cancer can affect any part of the mouth, including the lips, tongue, cheeks and throat, and has a number of characteristic symptoms, including ulcers that do not heal within three weeks, red and white patches or unusual lumps or swellings in the mouth. A major problem with being able to diagnose and treat mouth cancer is that many people displaying symptoms will ignore them for a long time, thereby delaying effective treatment.

What role do dentists play in relation to mouth cancer?

Early detection of mouth cancer is one of the key factors in successful treatment, a message that is reinforced by the annual Mouth Cancer Action Month campaign (www.mouthcancer.org). This means that regular screening by dentists plays a vital role in the process of diagnosing and treating those with the disease. This further supports the idea that dentists are responsible not just for treating teeth; they are in fact involved in every aspect of oral health.

What is the incidence of mouth cancer?

According to Cancer Research UK, there were nearly 12,061 new cases of head and neck cancer diagnosed in 2013. Head and neck cancer includes all forms of cancer found in the mouth, the nasal cavities and the larynx. Perhaps the most worrying statistic is that the incidence of the disease has increased 31% since the early 1990s.

Who is at risk?

There are a number of risk factors associated with mouth cancer. However, chewing tobacco or another similar product is the main risk, with excessive alcohol consumption, poor diet and the human papilloma virus (HPV) also being contributing factors. Smoking and drinking to excess is a particular problem because alcohol can aid tobacco absorption in the mouth. This can increase the risk up to thirtyfold.

Antibiotic resistance

Antibiotic resistance is the ability of pathogenic bacteria to resist the action of antibiotics, and it continues to be a major threat to all areas of medicine, including dentistry. Resistance is driven by the overuse and over-prescription of these drugs, both to humans and in agriculture, and in the long term has the potential to render all currently known antibiotics useless.

It is unclear what the future holds in relation to the use of antibiotics, but there is consensus that unless new drugs are discovered or alternative methods of treatment are developed, there will be a massive impact on our ability to successfully treat common infections and carry out invasive treatments that rely on the use of antibiotics.

Tooth whitening regulation

In recent years, there has been a large increase in the number of unregulated tooth whitening treatments administered to the general public. Thousands of people each year have this type of treatment carried out in beauty salons, shopping centres and high streets by individuals with no formal training in tooth whitening. A large increase in the number of complaints made against such companies has led the GDC to call for tooth whitening treatments to be more tightly regulated. The position of the GDC is now that any sort of cosmetic intervention to improve the whiteness of teeth is considered to be a dental treatment and as such should only be administered by a dentist or other regulated dental professional, such as a hygienist. It is therefore illegal for an organisation to carry out tooth whitening if there is not a suitably qualified dental professional present. Home whitening kits are still available, but because of the potential risks involved, they are also considered to be potentially dangerous and should be avoided.

The law currently states that tooth-whitening products containing between 0.1%–6% hydrogen peroxide should not be made directly available to the consumer and can only be administered by a dental professional to a patient over 18 years of age. Any products with greater than 6% hydrogen peroxide are illegal and anything containing under 0.1% can be sold directly to the consumer.

Tooth whitening is often carried out to improve the appearance of teeth if staining has occurred due to smoking, drinking tea, coffee and red wine, or just due to age. Common treatments involve using a bleaching gel to make this improvement, but if incorrectly done, this can result in problems such as removing the enamel from teeth and causing gum damage, hence why only qualified dental professionals can carry out treatments of this type.

The recent history of NHS dentistry in England

The history of NHS dentistry in the last decade is complex and to fully understand the current landscape, it is necessary to go back to the sweeping reforms of 2006 as a starting point.

What were the 2006 reforms?

In April 2006, the government carried out sweeping reforms of the system, which were heralded as a new dawn for NHS dentistry and were designed to entice more dentists into the service, thereby improving access to dental care. Under the old system, dentists were paid for each treatment they performed (there were around 400 separate charges), whereas the current system gives dentists a guaranteed income for providing a certain number of courses of NHS treatment to any patient requiring care. The reforms also targeted the pricing system and simplified the structure into three bands as follows:

- **Band 1:** covers an examination, diagnosis and advice. If necessary, it also includes X-rays, a scale and polish and planning for further treatment.

- **Band 2:** covers all treatment covered by Band 1, plus additional treatment, such as fillings, root canal treatment and removing teeth (extractions).
- **Band 3:** covers all treatment covered by Bands 1 and 2, plus more complex procedures, such as crowns, dentures and bridges.

Source: www.nhs.uk/common-health-questions/dental-health/what-is-included-in-each-nhs-dental-band-charge

Note that in this system, only one dental charge is incurred even if you need to visit more than once to complete a course of dental treatment. If you need more treatment at the same charge level (e.g. an additional filling) within two months of seeing your dentist, this is also free of charge.

The box below shows a more detailed breakdown of different costs as they stand at this point in time. Although the costs have changed over the past 12 years, the general structure of charges remains the same. You will see that all of the procedures listed fit into one of the three bands. A person pays only once – one charge for each course of treatment. For example, for a check-up, X-ray, teeth polish, a simple filling and a crown, a patient would pay a total of £233.70 if they all occurred within a two-month period. This pricing structure was designed to try to bring an end to the so-called 'drill and fill' culture and allow dentists to spend more time promoting preventive dentistry.

Dental procedure costs

Band 1 dental treatment: £21.60

This covers one or more treatments (as many as are necessary) from the following list:

- advice on preventing future problems, such as diet advice and cleaning instructions
- adjusting false teeth (dentures) or orthodontic appliances, such as braces
- applying sealants or fluoride preparations to the surfaces of your teeth
- a clinical examination, assessment and report
- marginal correction of fillings
- moulds of your teeth – for example, to see how your teeth bite together
- an orthodontic assessment and report
- a scale and polish (if clinically necessary)
- coloured photographs
- taking a sample of cells or tissue from your mouth for examination
- treating sensitive cementum (the tissue that covers the root of a tooth)
- X-rays.

Emergency treatment (when you need to see a dentist immediately) also costs £21.60.

Band 2 dental treatment: £59.10

This can cover anything listed in band 1 above, plus any of the following:

- an addition to your dentures – such as adding a clasp or a tooth
- apicectomy – removing the tip of the root of a tooth

- a mouth guard to correct your 'bite' (doesn't include a laboratory-made appliance)
- fillings
- free gingival grafts – when healthy tissue from the roof of your mouth is attached to your teeth where the root is exposed
- frenectomy or frenotomy – surgery to the folds of tissue that connect your tongue, lips and cheeks to your jaw bone
- treatment for severe form of gum disease – such as root planing (cleaning bacteria from the roots of your teeth),deep scaling and a polish, or a gingivectomy (removal of gum tissue)
- oral surgery – such as removing a cyst, or soft tissue surgery to the mouth or lips
- pulpotomy – removing dental pulp (the soft tissue at the centre of a tooth)
- relining and rebasing dentures
- removing teeth (extraction)
- root canal treatment
- sealant to fill small holes and seal any grooves in your teeth
- splinting loose teeth – for example, after an accident (this doesn't include laboratory-made splints)
- transplanting teeth.

Band 3 dental treatment: £256.50

This can cover anything listed in bands 1 and 2 above, plus any of the following:

- bridges – a fixed replacement for a missing tooth or teeth
- crowns – a type of cap that completely covers your real tooth
- dentures
- inlays, pinlays and onlays – used to restore damaged teeth
- orthodontic treatment and appliances such as braces
- other custom-made appliances, not including sports guards
- veneers and palatal veneers – new surfaces for the front or back of a tooth

Treatments such as veneers and braces are only available on the NHS if there's a clinical need for them (not for cosmetic reasons).

Source: www.nhs.uk/common-health-questions/dental-health/what-is-included-in-each-nhs-dental-band-charge

Reprinted with kind permission from NHS Choices

How were the reforms received?

When the reforms were introduced, many patients welcomed the changes because they felt they would go some way to resolving certain problems associated with accessing NHS dental care, in addition to making the pricing structure clearer. However, the changes did mean that the cost of some basic treatments increased.

Practising dentists were more sceptical of the reforms: a survey of dentists carried out by the BDA in the wake of the changes revealed that 55% of dentists did not think that they allowed them to see more patients. Before the reforms, according to the BDA, 32% of dentists performed 95% of their work on NHS patients, but this fell to 25% of dentists since the reforms. The reforms led to more than 1,000 dentists walking away from NHS work.

What was the impact of the reforms?

On the whole, the impact of the reforms was initially perceived to be negative, with a number of statistics and comments backing this up. Perhaps the most damning statistic that came to light following the reforms was that, in the two years following their introduction, 1 million fewer patients visited an NHS dentist. In addition to this, according to the BDA, 85% of dentists did not feel that the reforms had improved access. A report from the House of Commons Health Committee also stated that the reforms had not solved the 'fundamental problems'. It had also been implied that some dentists were less inclined to perform more complex treatments such as crowns and bridges because they received less money for them.

The BDA said the reforms did not give dentists enough time to do preventive work. This caused strong feelings among dentists, so much so that in some areas up to three-quarters of dentists threatened to quit the NHS. According to the BDA, the deal meant that dentists had to carry out 95% of the courses of treatment which they previously did to get the same money, thus leaving little time for addressing the causes of poor oral health. One of the key issues was that some dentists 'used up' the number of courses they had been allocated prior to the end of the year. This ultimately meant that they had to turn away any extra patients as they had been given no further funding to treat them.

In spite of some of the negative feelings about the NHS dental reforms, it is important to consider the statistics in terms of patient care: in the 24-month period ending in June 2013, 2.8 million more patients had been seen by a dentist than at the historic low point in June 2008. Although this does not tell the whole story about the reservations that dentists had about the reforms, it does indicate that they were success-ful in increasing patient contact and so the reforms should in some lights be seen as having an overall positive impact.

The 2009 review

In 2009, an independent review of NHS dental services was published that made recommendations about the way forward for dental care in this country. Professor Jimmy Steele, Professor of Oral Health Services Research at Newcastle University, engaged with dental professionals, NHS staff, patients and patient representative groups to compile this review. One of the key changes proposed in the review was that the income of dentists was to be determined by three factors – patient list size, quality of care, and the number of courses of treatment rather than just carrying out a set number of courses. In addition to this, the report suggested that patients needed to be provided with better information about available NHS dentists and that the three-band pricing structure should be widened to 10 bands. The full report can be found at https://webarchive.nationalarchives.gov.uk/20130123200117/http://www.dh.

gov.uk/en/Publicationsandstatistics/Publications/PublicationsPolicy
AndGuidance/DH_101137.

Following the publication of this report, the government accepted the
recommendations 'in principle' and the Department of Health began to
pilot them from 2011. The pilot has aimed to focus on providing the
treatment that the patient needs and avoiding unnecessary interven-
tions as well as increasing access to dental services and focusing on
the oral health of children. In 2014, the findings of the pilot were published (https://assets.publishing.service.gov.uk/government/uploads/
system/uploads/attachment_data/file/282760/Dental_contract_
pilots_evidence_and_learning_report.pdf).

In January 2015, the findings of the pilot were used to propose a series
of prototype contracts to be trialled as the next stage of the reform process. At this point in time, the government has 76 practices currently
taking part in the Dental Prototype Agreement Scheme with each practice running one of the two prototype contracts.

The pace of reform continues to be very slow; it has now been 13 years
since the last major changes. This seems to be a deliberate strategy to
ensure that the new system is tried, tested and fit for purpose. Lord
Howe, who wrote the foreword to the document, said the following:

> 'I know that there has been frustration at the pace of reform. I
> understand this frustration but I hope there is understanding of
> why we have taken a measured approach. The reform we are
> proposing is ground breaking and, we believe, will enable primary
> dental services to best meet the changing oral health needs of the
> population.'

Fluoridation

Perhaps one of the biggest issues in dentistry in recent decades has
been the fluoridation of water supplies and the impact it has on oral
health. Although this issue has been around for a long time, it is still vital
that you understand what the background is to the debate and the arguments for and against fluoridation.

What is fluoride?

Fluorine is a naturally occurring gas. When fluorine forms a binary com-
pound with another element, this is known as a fluoride. Fluoride ions
are found in soil, fresh water and seawater, plants and many foods.

How does fluoride work?

Fluoride is beneficial to both developing and developed teeth, as it
decreases the risk of decay. Dental decay is caused by acids produced
by the plaque on our teeth, which react with the sugars and other carbo-

hydrates we eat. The acids attack the tooth enamel, which, after repeated attacks, will break down, allowing cavities to form. Fluoride acts by bonding to the tooth enamel, thereby reducing the solubility of the enamel in the acids. Fluoride also inhibits the growth of the bacteria responsible for tooth decay. There is also evidence that it helps repair the very earliest stages of decay by promoting the remineralisation of the tooth enamel. However, fluoride is not a cure-all and the risk of tooth decay can still be increased by other factors such as exposed roots, frequent sugar and carbohydrate consumption, poor oral hygiene and reduced salivary flow.

What is fluoridation?

Fluoride occurs naturally in our water supply at varying levels, usually below 1 part per million (ppm). Fluoridation is the process by which the amount of fluoride is adjusted to the optimum level that protects against tooth decay. Where fluoride is added, the natural level is increased to approximately 1ppm.

What are the benefits of fluoridation?

Initially, the main beneficiaries of fluoridated water supplies were thought to be children under the age of five years. In areas where the concentration of fluoride in water supplies is 1ppm, rates of decay and tooth loss in children are greatly reduced. High levels of tooth decay in children are generally associated with areas of social deprivation. This is a pattern repeated throughout the EU and the USA. The best dental health regions in the UK are the West Midlands, an area where over two-thirds of the population receive fluoridated water, and south-east England, which is predominantly an affluent area. The worst areas for dental health are those associated with higher levels of social deprivation, such as north-west England. Children living in socially deprived areas with non-fluoridated water supplies can suffer up to six times more tooth decay than those living in more affluent areas or those receiving fluoridated water supplies. For example, in the poorest communities of north-west England, as many as one in three children of pre-school age have had a general anaesthetic for tooth extraction, and in Glasgow tooth extraction is the most common reason for general anaesthesia for children under the age of 10.

Research has shown that it is not only children who benefit from fluoridated water supplies but people of all ages, as the effect of fluoride on the surface of fully developed teeth is thought to be even more important. Elderly people in particular can benefit from drinking fluoridated water. The decrease in salivary flow with age, combined with reduced manual dexterity, means that it is more difficult to keep your teeth clean as you get older. So older people are more prone to root surface decay, which is difficult to treat. As fluoride strengthens adult tooth enamel, it helps reduce the incidence of this type of decay.

It is estimated that the NHS could save approximately £4 million per year on removal of rotten teeth in hospitals if fluoridation was extended to areas around the country with particularly high levels of tooth decay; this gives a potential economic benefit to fluoridation in addition to the benefits to oral health outlined above.

Probably the two most important advantages of fluoridated water supplies, as opposed to any other method of combating tooth decay, are that it is cost-effective and, more importantly, all members of the community are reached, regardless of income, education or access to dental care.

What are the problems with fluoridation?

The only proven side-effect of drinking fluoridated water is dental fluorosis. This is mottling of the teeth caused by a disruption of the enamel formation while the teeth are developing under the gums. It occurs between birth and the age of five years, when the enamel is developing. In mild cases, dental fluorosis is purely a minor cosmetic problem, which is barely visible to either the individual or the observer. It is also thought that mild dental fluorosis may further increase the resistance of the tooth enamel to decay. In moderate to severe cases of dental fluorosis, the colouring of the teeth is very pronounced and irregularities develop on the tooth surface. Whether this is purely a cosmetic problem or whether it adversely affects the function of the teeth is a matter of some debate.

Some research has claimed links between fluorosis and higher instances of bone cancer, osteoarthritis and fractures. However, numerous studies have concluded that there is no clear evidence that fluoridation of water at the recommended level of 1mg of fluoride to every litre of water causes harm to health, apart from dental fluorosis.

Other concerns expressed about fluoridation are its effect on the environment, particularly on plants. Fluorides have been used in some pesticides and insecticides and their use is now restricted. Other industrial fluorides are one of the main pollutants in waterways and the atmosphere.

What are the ethical issues involved in fluoridation?

One of the main ethical issues with fluoridation of water supplies involves infringement of personal liberty, as it effectively medicates everyone without an individual having the choice to refuse. We have no choice over our drinking water supply other than through our water company, unless we opt to buy bottled water, the cost of which would be prohibitive for certain sections of the community.

The issue of adding fluoride remains an emotive topic, as demonstrated when the decision was made to fluoridate the water supply of Southampton in 2008. The local health authority decided to introduce fluoridation in an attempt to reduce levels of tooth decay in the city. This plan was carried out in spite of a public consultation that suggested that 72% of 10,000 local people were opposed to the plan. As a result, local residents mounted a legal challenge, which had the backing of local politicians. Their opposition was based on 'the continuing uncertainties with regard to the long-term health risks associated with fluoridation' and 'the possible adverse environmental effects'. By October 2014, the proposed fluoridation plan had been scrapped in its entirety due to the opposition. Public Health England (PHE) said that it still endorsed fluoridation but could not proceed without the backing of the local council.

What is the situation in the UK?

In the UK, around 10% of water supplies are fluoridated. Approximately 6 million people receive optimally fluoridated water, around 3.5 million of whom live in the West Midlands area. Other areas with fluoridated supplies are East Midlands, the North East, Cumbria, Cheshire, Lincolnshire, Humberside and Bedfordshire.

The Water Act 2003 handed the decision of whether to fluoridate water supplies to the strategic health authorities (SHAs) in England and the health boards in Scotland and Wales. Following the abolition of SHAs, the power was devolved back to the individual local authorities, which now have the final say with regard to fluoridation.

The areas in most need of fluoridated water supplies are those with high tooth decay rates, including Merseyside and other parts of north-west England, Yorkshire, Scotland, Wales and Northern Ireland, plus some socially deprived communities in the south, such as inner London.

Who supports water fluoridation in the UK?

- British Medical Association
- Department of Health and Social Care
- BDA
- British Association for the Study of Community Dentistry (BASCD)
- British Fluoridation Society (BFS)
- World Health Organization (WHO)
- FDI World Dental Federation

What is the situation in other parts of the world?

According to the BFS, the USA has the most well-developed artificial fluoridation programme in the world, with approximately 171 million people receiving optimally fluoridated water. Other countries with fluoridated supplies are Canada, Brazil, Chile, Argentina, Peru, Guatemala, Guyana, the Irish Republic, Spain, Australia, New Zealand, Singapore, Malaysia, Brunei, South Korea, Vietnam, Papua New Guinea and Fiji.

What other products have fluoride added?

Several other methods of increasing fluoride intake have been used, including toothpaste, mouthwash, milk and salt. Salt fluoridation was first introduced in Switzerland in 1955 and is widespread in France, Switzerland, Germany, Spain, Austria, Hungary and the Czech Republic. This method has the advantage of not requiring a centralised piped water system and gives individuals control over its consumption.

However, it is not without its problems: dosage must take into account the other sources of fluoride in the area, to ensure that intake is not excessive. The production of fluoridated salt also requires specialist technology. Another consideration is the link between the consumption of sodium and hypertension, which would make this method of fluoride intake unsuitable for some individuals.

Fluoridated milk is also available and has been used widely (with parental permission) since 1993 in primary schools. Over 40,000 children in the UK, predominantly in the north-west of England, receive fluoridated milk at school, which has a concentration of 0.5mg of fluoride per carton. More recently, in 2016, Blackpool Council rolled out a plan to make fluoridated milk available for free to all primary school children as part of their breakfast clubs.

Another problem is monitoring and controlling fluoride administered in this manner; it is more difficult than with water because of the number of dairies involved. Fluoridated milk's dosage of fluoride also has to be adjusted, depending on whether the water supply is already naturally fluoridated or not. Additionally, a significant number of people do not drink milk for health or other reasons.

Mercury fillings

What are mercury fillings?

Amalgam fillings (the silver-coloured type) are the most common type of metal fillings and have been used for around 150 years. They are made of a combination of mercury (50%), silver (35%), tin (15%), copper and other metals. The major benefit of using amalgam is that it is economical, hard wearing and long lasting, and as such is ideal for using on molars.

Are there any risks associated with this type of filling?

There has always been a belief that mercury could not escape from the amalgam, but there is some evidence that mercury vapour does escape. Some countries have banned the use of mercury in fillings, among them Sweden and Austria. Critics of mercury in fillings claim that the vapour can cause gum disease, kidney, liver and lung problems, Alzheimer's disease and multiple sclerosis. However, according to the British Dental Health Foundation, dental amalgam containing mercury is not poisonous when combined with the other metals present. It states that: 'Research into the safety of dental amalgam has been carried out for over 100 years. So far, no reputable controlled studies have found a connection between amalgam fillings and any medical problem.'

What are the alternatives?

The British Society for Mercury Free Dentistry recommends the removal of amalgam fillings and their replacement by composite fillings, but only if precautions are taken to ensure that mercury is not ingested or inhaled during removal. 'White' fillings – made of composite materials or polymers – can be used in place of silver fillings, but they are not as strong and so can often be unsuitable for the back teeth, which are subjected to greater stress than the front teeth.

'Was my treatment necessary?'

Because dentists are paid for the treatment they perform, the more treatment that a patient receives or the more complex the treatment is, the more money the dentist will be able to charge. The question has therefore been raised as to whether dentists provide unnecessary treatment to patients just to make more money. The *Guardian*, in an article entitled 'Do dentists put the bite on patients?', carried out an experiment (albeit a limited one) to test this: a reporter booked examinations at a number of surgeries in London, and the recommendations ranged from one filling and a trip to the hygienist (cost then £32.92) to two fillings and three replacement crowns (£915 then). Even bearing in mind that dentists have to use their professional judgement as to whether treatment is urgently required or could be delayed, the range of recommended treatment in this particular instance is staggering.

There have also been suggestions that some NHS dentists can purposely stretch out a course of treatment over more than two months to make more money. Under the current contract, if patients have to return to the dentist within two months to finish a course of treatment or have further treatment, the work is covered by one fee. However, if the treatment goes beyond two months, the dentist would be able to charge again. One Welshman carried out a series of attacks on his dental surgery, including leaving a hoax bomb on its front doorstep, because he thought he had been overcharged by his dentist!

In spite of these concerns and potential issues, it is clear that the great majority of dentists are scrupulous about providing only appropriate treatment in an appropriate timeframe to their patients.

Treatments of the future

Over the past 30 years, the way we have looked after our teeth has improved vastly. We visit the dentist more often, spend more money on dental hygiene products and invest in a wide range of cosmetic dentistry procedures to make our teeth more aesthetically pleasing. As with any other scientific discipline, new treatments and practices are introduced as time goes on and these further improve dental and oral care, and consequently dental health and hygiene. Some recent examples are introduced below.

3D printing

Three-dimensional printing has improved rapidly in the past decade and the use of this technology is increasingly being incorporated into medical treatments, although it is still in its infancy in the dental world. This type of printing has the potential to create items such as crowns, veneers or implants specifically for an individual patient, but could also be used to make bespoke specialist tools to be used in certain procedures. While this technology is not currently used as standard, in the long term it has the potential to be used by dentists in providing routine treatments on a daily basis.

Smart toothbrushes

As an extension of the various smart devices that we use within our homes, electric toothbrushes seem to be the next gadgets due for a smart overhaul. The idea behind this is that the toothbrush connects to your smartphone and monitors the duration, frequency and quality of brushing you carry out each day. This technology is extremely useful to provide guidance and tips to help an individual to brush more effectively and could be a vital weapon in helping to improve oral health, particularly in younger people.

It is worthwhile trying to keep up to date with advances such as these by reading relevant newspapers, journals and websites. This will enable you to have a good understanding of where the profession is heading and give you the best possible chance of shining at interview.

7| Non-standard applications

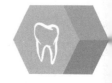

Most students who consider pursuing dentistry at university will be classified as 'standard' applicants: these would usually be UK residents studying chemistry and biology at A level, Pre-U, International Baccalaureate, or at Higher Level in Scotland. However, if you do not fit the profile of a 'standard' applicant but wish to study dentistry, there are other possible entry options that can be pursued.

Those who have not studied science at A level

If you decide that you would like to study dentistry after starting on a combination of A levels that does not fit the subject requirements for entry to dental school, or if you meet certain contextual factors related to the school you studied at or the area you live in, you may be eligible to apply for the pre-dental course.

The application procedure, the interview and UCAT requirements are the same as for the five-year course at that particular university.

This course is offered at five faculties of dentistry: Bristol, Cardiff, Dundee, Liverpool and Manchester (see Table 7 opposite for specific details). The course at Bristol is unique as it is aimed predominantly at students who have studied either biology or chemistry at A level but are unlikely to achieve the required grades due to contextual factors relating to the area they live in or the school they have previously studied at. At the other faculties the course is aimed predominantly at students who have only studied one science at A level and are predicted to secure AAA. The course covers elements of chemistry, biology and physics and lasts one academic year. Following successful completion, you automatically move on to the first year of the undergraduate dental course.

If your pre-dental application is unsuccessful, the best option is to take one-year science A level courses at a sixth-form or further education college. However, covering A level Biology and Chemistry from scratch in one year and getting the required A grades is a very tough challenge and should only be attempted by the most able students. You should discuss your particular circumstances with the staff at a number of colleges to select the course that will prepare you to achieve the A level subjects you need at the grades you require.

Table 7 Pre-dental course entry requirements – 2019/20

University	Standard offer	GCSE requirements	A level subject requirements	UCAT policy	Course code
Bristol	BBC	B in Science, Mathematics and C in English language	B in Biology or Chemistry	Required	A208
Cardiff	AAA	A/7 in English language and the single sciences or double award	Nor more than one science from Biology, Chemistry or Physics	Required	A204
Dundee	AAA	No specific/ minimum requirements BUT would take into account high GCSE grades (A*s)	No more than one science A level	Required	A204
Liverpool	-	Five at C or above to include Mathematics, English language and Science (requirements currently under review)	This course is designed for mature and non-traditional students who have taken a break from their studies for five or more years. It is not designed for A level students, school leavers or graduates	Not required	0AAW
Manchester	AAA	B in English language and Mathematics and double award Science, or C for separate sciences	Should predominantly be in Arts or Humanities subjects and should not include Biology and Chemistry	Required	A204

Overseas students

The competition for the few places available to overseas students is fierce and you would be wise to discuss your application informally with the dental school before submitting your UCAS application. Many dental schools give preference to students who do not have adequate provision for training in their own countries. You should contact the dental schools individually for advice.

According to the UCAS entrance statistics, students applying from outside the UK are much less successful than their UK counterparts in getting offers to study dentistry. For entry in 2017, 90 overseas students (EU and non-EU) gained a place to study at British universities, out of 1,415 applications. This represents a 6% chance of success compared with a 12% chance for UK students who applied in the same year. Further breakdown of these figures shows that in 2017, just 4% of applicants from the EU (excluding the UK) were successful, while non-EU international applicants had a 7% success rate.

In the aftermath of the EU referendum in June 2016, it now seems more likely that EU students will be treated in a similar way to non-EU international students in the future, particularly in terms of the fees they pay. This may lead to a reduction of EU applicants.

At the time of writing, the government has promised that EU students starting their studies in September 2019 will be charged the same fees as domestic students for the duration of their course. However, there have been no decisions made about the long-term fee status of EU students after Brexit and the picture is only likely to be clear after Brexit Day on 29 March 2019.

Qualifications

Many overseas students are applying with qualifications that are not equivalent to A levels or other UK qualifications. These students cannot be considered unless they have done a course that leads to qualifications recognised as being equivalent to A levels, such as the International Baccalaureate (IB) or the Irish Leaving Certificate. The dental schools' websites will quote entrance requirements in terms of A levels, IB, Scottish Highers, the Irish Leaving Certificate and other equivalent qualifications. If you are studying for other qualifications, you will need to contact the dental schools directly to ask their advice; this will give you a definitive answer about whether what you have been studying is suitable.

If your qualifications are not recognised you will need to think about following a one-year A level programme (studying Biology, Chemistry and another subject) and applying while studying. Students will also need to demonstrate a certain proficiency in English.

English language requirements

All overseas students are expected to demonstrate that they have a certain standard of English before commencing a dentistry course. This is most commonly demonstrated by using the International English Language Testing System (IELTS), although there are other qualifications that may be considered. Again, if you are unsure about the suitability of any English language qualification you must check directly with the university.

Each university independently sets its own IELTS requirements, which are clearly shown alongside its admissions information. This can be found on the university websites and also on the UCAS website. The requirements vary, but on average, most universities require an overall score of between 6.0 and 7.0, with scores in each individual section of between 6.0 and 7.0. For example, for 2018 entry, Birmingham and Liverpool required a minimum overall score of 7.0 with a minimum of 7.0 in each component.

The application form

Students who are studying outside the UK are often at a disadvantage because they may not have access to advisers at their schools who are familiar with the requirements of a successful UCAS application. The two areas that tend to be weakest are the personal statement and the reference.

Students who are unfamiliar with UCAS applications often write unsuitable personal statements that concentrate too much on non-essential information (prizes, awards, responsibilities) and not enough on matters relevant to dentistry. It is important to explain why you wish to study dentistry in the UK rather than in your home country. Detailed advice on the personal statement can be found in Chapter 5 of this book. Similarly, your referee needs to be familiar with what the dental schools require in the reference; I have seen numerous references written by academic advisers outside of the UK that are more like character references and therefore contain mostly irrelevant details. The UCAS website is a wealth of information, in relation to both personal statement and reference writing; particularly useful are the short videos that outline the key points about writing both of these documents. It is well worth ensuring that your chosen referee is familiar with this information before proceeding. Tips on writing the personal statement and reference can be found at www.ucas.com/undergraduate/applying-university/how-write-ucas-undergraduate-personal-statement.

Work experience

Dental schools always require applicants to have gained some relevant work experience, and often to have done some voluntary work as well, even if you are classed as a non-standard applicant. Work experience tells the selectors that the candidates are serious about becoming dentists and that they are familiar with what the profession demands. Voluntary work demonstrates that the applicant has the caring nature necessary to work with patients. Gaining work experience can be difficult, but you should make every effort to do so. If it is impossible for you to gain dental work experience, you might try to substitute it with hospital work or by attending relevant lectures. It is important that the reference explains why there is no mention of work experience in the application, and what you did to try to get that experience.

In addition to trying for work experience, there are short courses run at universities giving an insight into the demands of the course and profession. This is particularly useful for those who are not convinced that dentistry is the right profession for them, and also for those who have made up their minds but want greater insight and a good talking point for interview. Visit sites such as www.unitasterdays.com for further information on these short courses.

Interviews

Most dental schools require students to attend interviews. This is often difficult to arrange for students who are not based in the UK. It is worth contacting the schools before you apply to see whether they are likely to require you to travel to the UK to be interviewed. It is unlikely that there will be the option to be interviewed via Skype, particularly where the interview is in MMI format.

Quotas

While there is currently no restriction on places for EU students, who will be considered alongside UK applicants (although this may change post-Brexit), the UK government imposes quotas for non-UK/EU students. In general, students from countries that do not have adequate training programmes for dentistry are likely to have an advantage. If you are serious about studying dentistry in the UK, then do not be put off by the statistics. It is worth bearing in mind that while almost all of the UK applicants will be suitably qualified to study dentistry and will be aware of the entrance requirements (academic and other), a high proportion of overseas applicants will be rejected simply because they have not researched the requirements properly. So, careful preparation will give you a good chance of being considered.

While there has been some fluctuation in the numbers of EU and non-EU students being accepted to study dentistry over the past 10 years, in reality, the figures have remained relatively constant. For non-EU applicants, this has been somewhere between 50 and 80 acceptances per year, with 75 being the most frequent number. For EU applicants, this has been between 5 and 15 acceptances per year, with 10 being most frequent. The lack of variation in the numbers illustrates well the fact that there are strict quotas in place.

Mature students

Every year, there are a number of entrants to dentistry who are mature students. In 2017, there were around 2,210 applications to study dentistry from students aged 21 or over; 245 of these were accepted. In general there are three types of mature student:

1. those who have always wanted to study dentistry but failed to get into dental school when they applied from school in the normal way
2. those who have studied a science-related degree and at some point decided that they wish to study dentistry
3. those who came to the idea later on in life, often having embarked on a totally unrelated degree or career.

The first two types of applicant will usually have completed a degree in an associated discipline, such as a science- or healthcare-related subject, and usually will have obtained a minimum classification of 2.i. They may not have got into a dental school when they applied as an A level student, or perhaps they wanted to pursue a science degree without ever really considering dentistry at the time. Mture students will have a greater chance of success if they have pursued an appropriate biomedical or healthcare-related first degree, such as:

- anatomy
- biomedical sciences
- biochemistry
- human biology
- medical science
- physiology.

This is intended as a guide only, and the suitability of any degree course should be checked directly with the university.

This type of applicant would then apply to either a standard five-year course or a four-year graduate-entry course following completion of their first degree. The four-year course is offered by Aberdeen, Central Lancashire (UCLan), King's and Liverpool. These courses offer exemption from the first year of the course, so entry is into year two. Students who opt for this path can face an uphill struggle to make a successful application and so would need to have an excellent profile that demonstrates ongoing commitment to dentistry to maximise their chances of being accepted. Table 8 on page 118 gives details of these courses.

The third category of mature student is of equal interest to the dental school selectors and interviewers. Applications from people who have achieved success in other, non-science-related careers and who can bring a breadth of experience to the dental school and to the profession are welcomed. The main difficulty facing those who come late to the idea of studying dentistry is that they rarely have scientific backgrounds. There are two possible pathways that can be considered if you are in this position. Firstly, it would be possible to study science A levels and apply for a five-year course. Independent sixth-form colleges would be best placed to provide this pathway. Alternatively, it would be possible to apply to one of the six-year dental courses that incorporate a pre-dental year. Out of the five courses of this type that are available, Cardiff, Dundee, Liverpool and Manchester are open to

Table 8 Entry requirements for graduate courses – 2019/20

University	Pre-degree requirements	Degree requirements	Interview	UCAT policy	Course code
Aberdeen	None	At least 2.i in a medical or health-related science degree. Applicants with a first degree in medicine will also be considered.	Yes	Required	A201
King's	None	At least 2.i in a biosciences subject or a 2.ii in a biosciences subject or health professional subject with a post-graduate degree (with at least a merit).	Yes	Required	A202
Liverpool	A minimum of three A levels at grade ABB or above including Chemistry and Biology. The third subject may be from the arts or sciences. A minimum of seven GCSEs at grade B/6 or above, including Mathematics, English Language and a science subject. Vocational/Applied GCSEs are not accepted. Pending GCSE qualifications at the time of application are not accepted.	At least 2.i in a biosciences or helathcare-related degree subject.	Yes	Required	A201
University of Central Lancashire (UCLan)	Three A levels at C or above, including two from Biology, Chemistry, Physics and Mathematics. GCSE Mathematics and English Language at B/5.	2.i in a biomedical subject	Yes	Not required	A202

those who have achieved grades AAA at A level but have studied only a maximum of one science subject.

Case study: Utkarsh Dandekar, King's College London BDS 2

'I always knew that I wanted to be in a caring-based career as it's what gave me the most personal satisfaction when doing work experience. Having suffered from temporomandibular joint problems as a teenager, I was able to interact with my dentist on many occasions and soon saw how much the work of a dentist can change people's lives. It was this that ultimately confirmed my desire to pursue dentistry.

'Prior to applying to dentistry, I did work experience in various general dental surgeries in and around Birmingham. I also spent time in a hospital at the Maxillofacial Surgery Department at University Hospital Coventry. I volunteered for the NHS by delivering workshops on oral health to the community in and around East London. This helped me to appreciate the vital traits of a dentist and just how well you need to manage people's expectations.

'I initially studied a BSc in Biomedical Sciences, so did not go directly into the world of dentistry. It was only following the completion of my degree and taking a gap year that I finally decided to apply. I felt that my initial undergraduate study, coupled with my year out, gave me great opportunities to develop as a learner and as a person. All of my experiences strengthened my application and I was lucky enough to secure a place to study dentistry at King's College London (KCL) on the five-year course.

'My first year at KCL was spent covering most of the basic biomedical sciences. Because I had already gained a BSc prior to starting dentistry, things were fairly straightforward. We did get some exposure to clinics and had opportunities to nurse for the seniors in the years above, which was great. At the end of the year, we started collecting real teeth to then create upper and lower jaws into which we would be drilling.

'I have just started my second year and this is the year where the bulk of the learning is done in terms of dentistry. So far, it is definitely a step up from last year in terms of the quantity of work. There are more 8.30am starts and the day can typically finish at around 4pm. Sometimes the workload can be a little overwhelming, and it is important that prospective students are well aware of the demands. I tend to cope by staying organised and managing my time carefully. I also tend to engage myself in extracurricular activities, and thrive on doing lots of things.

'Even though the course is demanding, the Dental Society at KCL is very proactive in organising an array of social events, giving everyone from the staff and students a chance to get involved. The talks are inspiring, with many famous people coming to KCL and speaking to us on topics in dentistry.

'My tips to prospective students are to:

'**Stay organised.** Every Sunday I will plan the next week to come and organise my calendar. Whether it's lectures, tutorials, seeing patients or even socialising, get organised and you'll soon realise that you'll manage your time a lot better.

'**Get an overview of lectures.** It's important to understand the concepts rather than just remembering the facts. University teaching is a lot different to college and some people may be overwhelmed with just how much content one lecture may have. Don't panic. Understand the concepts first and if you are really struggling, contact your personal tutor – they're there to help you.

'**Be proactive in your learning.** I always found revising in groups is a great way of testing one another. Use visual aids and a variety of resources. YouTube can be your friend (at times) and there are plenty of resources out there on the web.

'**Have a balance.** University and dental school is a wonderful opportunity to make friends, socialise and really enjoy your time before you start in the real world as a dentist. I can guarantee it that your time will go quickly – so make the most of it. Join societies. Play a sport. Do charity work. It'll all look great for when you're looking for a job. Network – especially with the staff and the years above. It's a great opportunity not only to know more dentists, but they'll usually have more hints and tips that will help you at dental school. In terms of networking, go to the BDSA events that happen annually. There is a conference and sports day, two of which are hosted by a different dental school each year. It's a great way of meeting other dental students around the country. The conferences are full of interesting dental talks in various fields and may spark a particular dental interest for you.

'**Be resilient.** Getting into dental school is challenging – it may even be the hardest thing that you do. Do not be disheartened if you don't get in on the first attempt. Pick yourself up, stay positive and keep trying. Remember that once you're in, it's the start of a long career. You'll constantly be faced with challenges from day one right through to when you retire. It's mentally, physically and emotionally challenging so do not expect an easy ride. Stay focused on what you want as a dentist and never lose sight of that.'

Case study: Jas Johal, second year BDS, studying at UCLan

'My passion for dentistry started as a teenager when I had braces and became interested in orthodontics. I've always been quite hands-on and wanted to do something science-based, so I decided to do some work experience at a local dentist to ensure dentistry was for me – and it was! I like the fact that dentists have the option of branching off and becoming specialists in fields that interest them most. I think the greatest lesson I learned from my work experience was how important it is for a dentist to communicate with the patient. I also used the opportunity to be certain that I was making the right decision about my future vocation; doing as much work experience as possible really helped me to make up my mind.

'My route into dentistry was through the graduate entry course at UCLan. I have a master's degree in osteopathy, so I was able to apply to the four-year course. Prior to applying, I completed a one-year A level Biology course as I hadn't studied it previously; I was lucky enough to secure an A*!

'So far, I am really enjoying the course, but it's really challenging! I constantly want to improve and do things better and this is one of my main driving forces for working hard. I particularly enjoy the hand-on elements of the course; in the first week we did our first composite (white) filling, which was awesome, and I loved working with the phantom head. There's also a good social side to dentistry and it's not just all work. The university dental society organises a lot of social events, as do the BDSA, which are amazing!

'In terms of challenges so far, the work is by no means easy. It's not that the work is particularly hard, it's just the volume of information can be a little overwhelming, but as long as you keep on top of it, it's not so bad.

'My tips to prospective dentists are to make sure you do lots of work experience and be enthusiastic when doing it. This will ensure you get the most out of the experience and you're more likely to enjoy it too! When coming for interviews, have a basic knowledge of different procedures and ethical issues as they like to ask these kinds of questions.'

Studying abroad

One option for those who have been unsuccessful with their applications is to study dentistry at one of a number of dental schools abroad. These are five- and six-year courses that are taught in English. There are a number of well-known universities, such as Charles University in the Czech Republic and Comenius University in Bratislava, that are found within the European Economic Area (EEA), but there are also numerous courses at institutions within the core European Union and outside Europe that are also taught in English. There is no central body like UCAS to apply through for these schools, so applications are completed individually for each dental school. The admissions process can differ for each university, but there may be the requirement to sit an entrance exam and/or attend an interview.

It is advised that students who are interested in studying abroad start their research up to 18 months in advance. This will allow enough time to thoroughly complete any application forms, sit any required tests or entrance exams (including language tests), obtain a visa (if required) and find funding. There are different guidelines to follow depending on where you wish to study and you will also need to research exactly what it is that you need to do. For example, if you wish to pursue a course within the EU and you are an EU national (which currently includes the UK), you have a right to study in any other EU country. You also have the right to be charged the same level of fees that a home student in that country would pay. This means that the process is relatively straightforward, and there is no requirement to apply for a visa. At this point, the final details of the Brexit agreement have not been decided, so how UK students will be treated after Brexit day is still unclear.

If you wish to study outside the EU, however, there may be a requirement to apply for a student visa. You may also find that you have to pay different fees compared to students who originate from the country. It is vital that you speak with the embassy or consulate of the country you wish to study in to check the steps that need to be followed.

There are some companies based in the UK that aim to help you gain entry to one of a number of these universities; however, it is best to approach the university directly to discuss entry as this is often a more straightforward and less expensive option. Applicants who are offered a place to study dentistry in Europe are not obliged to accept their place if they later choose to study in the UK. It is advisable for any committed prospective dentist who is applying for a UK dental school to have a back-up option to study dentistry in Europe, in the event that their application in the UK is unsuccessful.

When considering study abroad, you should remember that if you wish to come back to the UK to work as a dentist after graduation, you must first pass the Overseas Registration Exam (ORE) if you have studied outside of the European Economic Area (EEA). The ORE is designed to test knowledge and clinical skills based on the curriculum of UK dental schools. If you pass, you are then eligible to apply for full registration with the GDC, which will allow you to practise in the UK. Full details can be found at www.gdc-uk.org/professionals/ore. At the moment, if you studied in another EEA country (currently Austria, Belgium, Bulgaria, Croatia, Cyprus, Czech Republic, Denmark, Estonia, Finland, France, Germany, Greece, Hungary, Iceland, Ireland, Italy, Latvia, Liechtenstein, Lithuania, Luxembourg, Malta, The Netherlands, Norway, Poland, Portugal, Romania, Slovakia, Slovenia, Spain and Sweden) your qualification can allow you to register with the GDC as long as the course is approved by the regulator in whichever country you are studying in. The UK National Academic Recognition Information Centre (UK NARIC; www. naric.org.uk/naric/Individuals/Occupations/Dentists.aspx) can advise on regulations and outline the steps you may need to take before finding employment as a dentist in this country.

As has been previously mentioned, the June 2016 referendum on the UK's relationship with Europe has somewhat confused the situation in terms of studying in the EEA. At this point, the exact details of the future relationship between the UK and EU are still unclear, but it would be worth considering that as the UK's relationship with Europe changes, it may well alter the rules in terms of eligibility to return to practise dentistry in the UK after graduation.

Case study: Karan Maini, fifth year dentistry

'Dentistry had always been a passion of mine from a very young age. Although being a demanding career path, I always found the challenge it presented to be intriguing, and having now studied for four years in an international dental school, I can safely say it is more than rewarding. Learning a new language, culture and profession provided me with a rare opportunity that not many will be privileged to experience.

'Prior to applying, I was lucky enough to secure work experience in both private and NHS dental practices and soon learned that dentistry is not just looking at teeth. I also realised that there are a broad range of specialities in the dental field, and although I struggled to understand the technical terminology at this stage, I was able to appreciate that dentistry has many different aspects.

'Upon receiving my A level results, because I was in a situation where I had not secured a place to study in the UK, I searched for European universities that might accept me. After a few weeks of researching my options, I applied to study dentistry in Valencia, Spain. Pursuing this course at this particular university has been by far the best thing I have ever done, despite the long hours of studying, the countless exams and the need to be expending 100% effort all the time. During my time here, the positives really have outweighed the negatives and I've felt a real sense of accomplishment in reaching my final year knowing that all that hard work I have put in has been worth it.

'Studying abroad has been tough in many respects. There are different rules to follow, different types of people and different systems compared to the UK, but after the initial shock, it really doesn't take too long to get used to it. I believe that adapting to new situations is a massively important skill needed for dentistry, so in the long run, it has only helped me to become a better dentist.

'In Valencia, the lecturers and professors are meticulous when it comes to detail, and this has particularly appealed to me. I really feel that this level of scrutiny is good as it has helped me to develop skills that will distinguish me from other dentists. The only thing that I don't really enjoy is the sheer number of exams that we have, although I appreciate the need for ongoing assessment. I feel it would be more productive to have two large exams at the end of the semester as opposed to two or three for each individual subject.

'My advice for prospective applicants to dentistry: Be prepared. If your application is not successful, don't be disappointed, there are lots of possible routes into the profession. It definitely doesn't mean that you won't make a good dentist or that you are not capable of studying dentistry, it just means that you will have to work a little bit harder to prove to yourself that it's possible.'

Students with disabilities and special educational needs

Students with disabilities and special educational needs are welcome to apply to study dentistry. The vast majority of universities will have an equality and diversity adviser or team (or equivalent) that is employed to provide guidance and support to students with specific needs.

It is absolutely vital that any specific learning difficulty or disability be disclosed in the appropriate section of your UCAS application. It is crucial that no details be hidden from the university at this point. If the university knows about your needs from the start, it will be better placed to provide the appropriate support from the beginning of your course. It is also important to remember that your application will not be discriminated against based on the information you provide in it.

It must be remembered, however, that dentistry makes very specific physical demands on individuals. As a result, any physical disability that may interfere with the ability to meet these demands may make dentistry an unsuitable course. The GDC recommends that a student should only be accepted onto a course if he or she is able to carry out all of the tasks normally done by dentists. It also requires applicants to satisfy the 'fitness to practise' criteria. If you are unsure about how your disability will affect you in these areas, then it is worth contacting the universities so that you can be assessed individually.

It is also worth contacting the team at each university where you wish to study in advance of applying to discuss the facilities and mechanisms it would be able to put in place to support you during your studies. This is a vital task and so should form part of your research and fact-finding about a particular university.

8 | What do I do on results day?

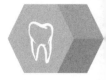

You will probably have been worrying about results day for a number of weeks by the time it eventually rolls around. Although it can be a very emotional day for some, it is important to be thoroughly prepared to deal with whatever situation may arise on the day.

Your A level results will usually arrive at your school on the third Thursday in August, with the dental schools receiving them sometime before this. Scottish Higher results are traditionally released a week earlier than A level results. It is vital that you are present in person on the day so that you can collect your results; don't wait for your school to post them, and try to avoid getting them by phone or email as this can sometimes lead to you being given incorrect information. Collecting your results at school will put you in the best position to act as quickly as possible if you haven't managed to secure your place. Prior to results day, check what time your school opens and what time results are available; the sooner you get to your school and pick them up, the sooner you could be on the phone to university admissions teams. In addition to this, you will be able to find out whether you have been accepted or rejected vy your chosen universities prior to going into your school or college by logging on to UCAS Track, so have your login details to hand.

If you received a conditional offer and your grades equal or exceed that offer, congratulations! You can relax and wait for your chosen dental school to contact you with details of accommodation and other arrangements.

What to do if you hold no offer

There are a number of students who will approach results day without having received an offer from a dental school. There are a small number of dentistry places each year allocated through Clearing, although these are unlikely to be formally advertised in the national press. It is extremely unlikely that a student will secure a place on a dentistry course in this way, but it is certainly not impossible, especially if your grades include at least one A* in a science subject. If you find yourself in this position, telephone all of the dental schools as soon as possible on results day to explain your situation. Although most are likely to say no, some universities have been known to invite students for interview on or shortly after results day and then subsequently make an offer. Remember the chances of this happening are slim, and most students will end up using Clearing to secure a place on an alternative course.

If you hold three A/A* grades but were rejected when you applied through UCAS (i.e. you did not get an offer), you need to let the dental schools know that you are out there, and discuss options for how you may secure a place in the future. The best way to do this is by phone or email, as these are the quickest ways of contacting the dental schools directly. It is always best to try to establish a good working relationship with admissions teams at the universities you are interested in, as they will be more likely to give you advice and help you in the future.

In this situation, the main option you have is to reapply through UCAS in the next admissions cycle. Although you will already have the grades for entry in this situation, it is important to understand that there are a number of other elements of your application that you'll need to work on to maximise your chances of securing a place. Things to consider are listed below.

- Your personal statement: revisit it and cast a critical eye over it. This is also an opportunity to add any work placements or other positive experiences that you have had since your last application.
- Your UCAT/BMAT score: you will need to resit any pre-admissions tests for each admissions cycle. This will give you a chance to complete further practice questions and learn from your experience of sitting it first time around. It may also be a good idea to attend one of the UCAT/BMAT preparation courses that are available.
- Your work experience and voluntary work: any opportunity to add further work experience to your profile will always be a good idea. Whether it is dentistry-related or just general voluntary work, it will have a positive impact.

What is UCAS Extra?

UCAS Extra is a service that allows students to apply to additional courses if they have been rejected by all their choices or declined all of their offers. This option is open between February and July and is a normal part of the whole application process. If at any time in the cycle you are eligible for UCAS Extra, it will show up when you log in to Track.

Since UCAS Extra started, I have not known any dentistry courses to be advertised, and I doubt that this will change in the future due to the continued high levels of demand for places. However, if you have been rejected from your first-choice courses, Extra provides an excellent opportunity to apply for other alternative courses without having to go through Clearing.

If you wish to use this facility, you must first search through the available courses on the UCAS website to find one that you are interested in and then call the university to check that it will consider you. If it gives you a positive response, then you can add the details on Track; the university will then contact you in the usual way when it has considered your application. If you do opt to use Extra, you will only be able to apply for one course at a time; you will not be able to add multiple courses all at once.

Is UCAS Adjustment of any use to me?

In effect, the UCAS Adjustment option is designed to be a 'trading up' system for applicants who pass their exams with better results than expected. However, you can only enter Adjustment if your results have met and exceeded the conditions of your conditional firm choice. A student must have held a conditional firm choice on their application to be eligible, and so if you have had no offers it is not something you can use.

What to do if you hold an offer but miss the grades

If you have only narrowly missed the required grades, it is important that you contact the dental admissions team as soon as possible. As mentioned previously, you will probably know what their decision is at this point, thanks to the UCAS website. If you have been rejected, it is vital that you keep a level head and do not panic; you must stay calm throughout. If you have not been rejected outright or are unsure of their decision, you must contact the admissions team by telephone – so ensure that in the run-up to results day you have gathered together the contact numbers of the universities you have accepted as your firm and insurance choices.

In some cases, dental schools will allow applicants who hold a conditional offer to slip a grade (particularly if they came across well at the interview stage) rather than offering the place to somebody else. However, be warned – this is by no means guaranteed, and most of the time dropping a grade will result in outright rejection, although the chances of being accepted in this position have improved in recent years.

When speaking to the universities, they are likely to give you a simple yes or no answer or tell you that you are still being considered. It is unlikely that crying, begging or pleading your case to the person on the phone will make any difference to the overall decision. If they tell you that you have been rejected, there are some questions you should ask.

- Would they consider your application if you applied next year (i.e. do they accept resit students)?
- What would the likely grade requirements be?
- Would they need to interview you again?
- Would they require you to resit the UCAT/BMAT? (Although the general policy is that it should be retaken, some universities have been known to waive this requirement.)

If they have given you a positive response about reapplying, seek to get it confirmed in writing, as this will give you hard evidence of their intention to consider your application again. It is probably easiest for them to confirm this by email, so you will first need to send them an email to enquire. If you are told by the universities you held offers with that they will not consider your application in the next cycle, you should call other dental schools to see if they would consider you. Unfortunately, the number of dental schools that will consider applications from retake students who have not held a conditional firm offer with them has becoming increasingly limited (see Table 4 in Chapter 3).

If you have had a positive response from one or more dental schools about reapplying, you would then need to consider retaking your A levels and applying again later in the year (see below). The alternative is to use the Clearing system to obtain a place on a degree course related to the biological/biomedical sciences and then apply to the dental course after you graduate and hope to be offered a place.

Retaking A levels

If you narrowly miss the required grades in your A levels after two years of study, you may wish to take the opportunity to retake any subject in which you underperformed to try to boost your grade. Remember that it is extremely difficult to make a successful application as a retake student, so improving your grades may not be enough to get you into dentistry. Before you embark on any retake courses, you need to carry out thorough research into which universities would consider you as a retake student. This information changes every year, so the only way to make sure that you have the most up-to-date information is to contact the university directly and explain your situation.

If you held offers with dental schools in the previous year and only narrowly missed your grades, you are more likely to be considered again the following year. For example, Cardiff University has recently made it easier for students who had put it as their firm choice to reapply if they narrowly miss the grade requirements.

Due to the recent reform of A levels, individual units can no longer be retaken. This means that if your final grade is below what you needed, you will have to retake all of the exams rather than just being able to target individual units, making it impossible to improve your grade by making minor adjustments to individual units.

Numerous state and independent sixth-form colleges provide specialist advice and teaching for students considering A level retakes. Interviews to discuss this are free and carry no obligation to enrol on a course, so it is worth taking the time to do this before you embark on A level retakes.

Case study: Puja Jalota, second year dentistry student at Cardiff University

'Originally I never imagined that I would get into dental school, but in September 2015, there I was at Cardiff University to begin the course.

'As much as I enjoyed learning biology and chemistry in my GCSE year, I really did struggle with the subjects and was always failing to finish tests in the time given. This would very much frustrate me as no matter how hard I tried, I always felt slow compared to my classmates. Nevertheless, I continued to work hard and surprised myself with a decent set of GCSE results.

'It was during my first year of A levels where I found out I was significantly dyslexic and had dyspraxia too. My struggles to complete work finally had an explanation. That year was the first time in my life where I managed to finish all of my exams, now with the extra time, to the best of my ability, with no anxiety or big panic attacks.

'I achieved an offer from Cardiff for dentistry the following year and was completely overjoyed. However, this was short-lived, as after a hard year's work my A2 results were A, B, C. I was distraught and had no clue what my future plans were at that point. I had a couple offers through Clearing for another course which many teachers were advising me to choose from. However, I decided I couldn't throw in the towel so easily and decided to take the year out and try again.

'I decided to re-sit biology and chemistry over the course of a year and by January I received confirmation that Cardiff University had given me a second chance with a dentistry offer there. My teachers were incredibly supportive during this year, encouraging and really helped to make me believe that I was capable of getting the grades I needed.

'Results day came around again and I had managed to secure an A* in biology and an A in chemistry. I cried I was so happy! I began university a totally different person. I was more mature but most importantly had greater self-belief.

'Initially I didn't enjoy the pressure and intensity of the course. I found in my first year of dentistry the pressure of staying on top of things was almost overwhelming. I was struggling to keep up with the large volume of content and assignments, as well as making sure I understood my work properly. However, as the year progressed, I became more accustomed to the demanding pressures and learnt to balance the workload and university life much better.

Although dentistry is a demanding course, it really feels like you are never struggling on your own. A fellow course mate will always be there to help, support and motivate you through any problem you are finding difficult to cope with.

'My biggest tip is to stay determined. This may sound clichéd, but in the grand scheme of things I feel it is the most crucial thing to keep in mind, not only when applying for dentistry or working towards achieving your A level grades, but also in the duration of the five years of the course and even afterwards. If you falter in anything once, twice, or more, don't let it stop you, you can do it.'

Reapplying to dental school

Most dental schools do not consider retake candidates (see Table 4 in Chapter 3), so the whole business of applying again needs careful thought and research, hard work and a bit of luck.

When reapplying, the choice of dental schools open to you will be much narrower than the first time round. Most do not consider retake students at all; others will only consider you if there are extenuating circumstances that affected your academic performance; while some will only consider you if you previously applied to study with them and were made an offer. It is vital that you check the advice given by each dental school before you think about applying to it, as their position on retake students is always changing.

If you feel that there are extenuating circumstances that have prevented you from reaching your target grades, you must try to get evidence to support this in advance of results day. For example, if you have had a medical condition that has affected your performance, a letter from your doctor will be sufficient. Some examples of acceptable reasons for underachieving are:

- your own illness
- the death or serious illness of a very close relative.

The following are examples of excuses that would not be regarded by admissions tutors as extenuating circumstances.

- 'I had so many exams to revise for that I didn't have time to do everything.'
- 'I have three young brothers and the noise they make stops me from revising.'
- 'I went skiing at Easter, and was unable to revise properly because it was too cold in the evenings for me to work.'
- 'I lost all of my notes a week before the exam and so couldn't revise.'

- 'We moved house a month before the exams, which disrupted my revision schedule.'

These are just guidelines, and the only safe method of finding out whether a dental school will consider your application is to call or write and ask. It is often worth writing an email or letter so that you have firm details of what has been discussed to refer back to at a later point if necessary. An example is provided below, although a telephone discussion could also take this form. Don't follow it word for word, and do take the time to write to several dental schools before you make your final choice. The format of your email should be:

- an opening paragraph
- your exam results: set them out clearly and with no omissions
- any extenuating circumstances (a brief statement)
- your retake plan, including the timescale
- a request for help and advice
- a closing paragraph.

Make sure that your letter is brief, clear and well presented. If you have had any previous contact with the admissions staff you will be able to write 'Dear Dr Smith' and 'Yours sincerely'. Even if you go to this trouble, the pressure on dental schools in the autumn is such that you may receive no more than a standard reply to the effect that, if you apply, your application will be considered. Apart from the care needed in making the choice of dental school, the rest of the application procedure is as described in the first part of this guide.

Remember that if you are reapplying to universities that use the UCAT/BMAT, then in all probability you will also have to resit the test, regardless of how you did in the previous year. Unfortunately, it is always your most recent score that counts, not your highest.

Dear Miss Nash

Last year's UCAS No. 08-123456-7

I am currently in the process of completing my UCAS application and am particularly interested in applying to your university to study dentistry. I applied to you last year and received an offer of AAB but missed the grades/was rejected after interview/was rejected without an interview. However, I am very impressed by the university and the structure of the course and as such would like to apply again. I have just received my A level results, which were Biology A, Chemistry B, Psychology B.

During my final year of A levels, I had significant health problems that prevented me from achieving the grades I am capable of. I am now embarking on retaking each of my subjects in order to improve my grades. Now that I am back to full health, I have no doubt that I can achieve A grades in each subject.

Could you please advise me as to whether you would consider my application, given the circumstances I have outlined above. I am very keen not to waste a slot on my UCAS application (or your time) by applying to you if you will reject me purely because I am retaking.

I am very keen to study here, and would be extremely grateful for any advice that you can give me.

Yours sincerely

Diana Littlewood (Miss)

9| Fees and funding

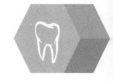

Whether undertaking an undergraduate or postgraduate course, the cost of studying is considerable. This has been exacerbated in recent years by rises in living costs and the large increases in university tuition fees following the publication of the Browne review in 2010. A 2017 study carried out by the Institute for Fiscal Studies (www.ifs.org.uk/publications/9335) calculated that average debt upon graduation was £42,500 per student, with students from the poorest backgrounds graduating with debt in excess of £57,000. However, these figures were based on an average of all students, rather than focusing on dental students. If we take into account the course length, then an English student at an English dental school in London could leave university with a significantly higher level of debt if the full amount of tuition fee and maintenance loan is received and there is no financial support from other sources. Bear in mind, however, that this overall cost to students will fluctuate depending on a number of factors. Some of these are listed below.

- Geographical location: obviously studying in London is going to be more expensive than studying in Birmingham.
- Area of permanent residence: there are differences in fees payable and help available depending on where you are from.
- Parental help: contributions from parents may significantly help meet the cost of living.
- Availability of scholarships: does the university offer scholarships for exceptional students?
- Finding a job: although it has the potential to interfere with your studies, working during your time at university will help to reduce the overall burden of debt.

When considering levels of student debt, it is easy to become disheartened and think that university study is not for you. I commonly hear students saying that they can't afford to go to university as they don't have the money to pay for it. What all students must remember is that tuition fees do not have to be paid up front; in fact, most students receive student loans to cover this cost. In addition, the loans do not start to be paid back until you are earning over a certain amount. The full details of this will be discussed later in the chapter.

Regardless of how much debt you incur, or how you fund your way through university, hopefully these figures will help you to realise that undertaking a course such as dentistry should only be done after seriously considering the overall cost and carefully examining your ability to be fully committed to your study for the full five years.

To find out what the fees are and what funding is available for dentistry courses, you should explore each of the universities' websites and/or talk to their financial departments, because fees and funding procedures vary from university to university. However, due to the high quality of education provided by dental schools, it is extremely likely that all of these courses will charge the maximum amount permitted.

It is vital to ensure that you carefully plan your finances in advance so that you are prepared to cover the cost of tuition fees, living expenses, books and other necessary equipment. Needless to say, living costs in big cities such as London will be much higher than in other parts of the country.

Fees

UK

Students who are UK nationals pay lower tuition fees than non-EU international students. From September 2018, universities have been able to charge up to £9,250 per year for tuition fees; it is expected that this figure will continue to rise in the future in line with inflation. The rise in fees is part of the government's new Teaching Excellence Framework (TEF), which assesses universities and colleges on the quality of their teaching. The institutions with a TEF award are able to charge £9,250, whereas those without a TEF award are only able to charge £9,000. Tuition fee loans have also increased to cover the higher fees.

There are a number of differences between the systems in England, Scotland, Wales and Northern Ireland, which can result in massive differences between the fees that are ultimately paid by students. From September 2018, the rules are as follows, although they may be subject to change in the future.

- English students are liable for the full fees being charged regardless of where they study within the UK, although for Welsh universities, the maximum amount being charged is still £9,000.
- Students living in Scotland who wish to study full time at a Scottish university are not required to pay tuition fees as long as eligibility criteria are met. Scottish students who wish to study at a university in England or Northern Ireland are required to pay fees of up to £9,250 per academic year. If studying in Wales they will pay £9,000 per year.
- For students residing in Wales, up to £9,250 per academic year will be payable if studying at an English, Scottish or Northern Irish university. Welsh students wanting to study in Wales have their fees subsidised by the Welsh Assembly and so are only required to pay up to £9,000 per year.

- Students living in Northern Ireland who wish to study in Northern Ireland will pay £4,160 per academic year. Northern Irish students who wish to study elsewhere in the UK are required to pay up to £9,250 per academic year for studying in England or Scotland and £9,000 for studying in Wales.

EU students

EU students, not including those living in the UK, can expect to pay different levels of fees depending on where they study in the UK. From September 2018, the rules are as follows.

- EU students studying in England will pay up to £9,250 per year, depending on the course.
- In Scotland, these students are not required to pay tuition fees as long as they meet eligibility criteria.
- In Wales, EU students pay up to £9,000 per year.
- In Northern Ireland, EU students pay £4,160 per academic year.

Following the June 2016 referendum result for the UK to leave the European Union, there has been a great deal of uncertainty regarding the future status of EU students studying in the UK. At this point, it is unclear exactly what the long-term impact will be, but it is possible that separate arrangements will need to be negotiated regarding the fees that EU students pay. In light of the post-referendum political landscape, it seems highly unlikely that EU students will be able to enjoy the parity they currently have with domestic students and as a consequence the fees that they pay may rise sharply.

Despite this uncertainty, funding arrangements for courses starting in September 2019 have been confirmed as outlined above. These arrangements will remain in place until the end of any course started at this point, regardless of what is agreed as part of the final Brexit deal.

Non-EU international students

For international students from outside the UK and EU, the costs of studying in the UK are significantly greater and can often be prohibitive. For example, at the University of Birmingham the tuition fees for students starting in the academic year 2019–20 will be £21,180 per annum for years 1 and 2, rising to £38,100 per annum for years 3, 4 and 5. At King's College London, international students will pay £43,500 per annum. While there is some variation in cost between universities, these fees are broadly representative of the whole of the UK.

Table 9 Annual tuition fees by region for courses starting in 2018

Student's home region	Studying in England	Studying in Scotland	Studying in Wales	Studying in Northern Ireland (2016*)
England	Up to £9,250	Up to £9,250	Up to £9,000	Up to £9,250
Scotland	Up to £9,250	No fee	Up to £9,000	Up to £9,250
Wales	Up to £9,250	Up to £9,250	Up to £9,000	Up to £9,250
Northern Ireland	Up to £9,250	Up to £9,250	Up to £9,000	Up to £4,160
EU	Up to £9,250	No fee	Up to £9,000	Up to £4,160
Other international	Variable	Variable	Variable	Variable

Source: www.ucas.com/ucas/undergraduate/finance-and-support/
undergraduate-tuition-fees-and-student-loans.
We acknowledge UCAS' contribution of this information.

Financial help

There are a number of sources of financial help that are potentially available for full-time students from both the UK and EU to help cover the cost of university study. The main ones are student loans and bursaries, which are all allocated according to individual and family circumstances. It is important to apply as soon as possible through the Student Finance online service in order to prevent delay in receiving this assistance. There are different Student Finance sites to use depending on which country you are a permanent resident of. These sites contain detailed information on the help that is available and how to apply for it:

- **England:** Student Finance – www.gov.uk/studentfinance
- **Scotland:** Student Awards Agency for Scotland (SAAS) – www.saas.gov.uk
- **Wales:** Student Finance Wales – www.studentfinancewales.co.uk
- **Northern Ireland:** Student Finance Northern Ireland – www.studentfinanceni.co.uk

For the most recent figures, please check the relevant Student Finance websites regularly.

Student loans

The most common way for students to finance their studies is by taking out a student loan. If you are an eligible, full-time student, you can take out two types of loan: a loan for tuition fees and a maintenance loan to meet living costs. The tuition fees loan does not depend on your household income and is paid straight to the university to cover the full cost. You can borrow all or part of the amount required to cover your fees.

The amount of maintenance loan you are entitled to depends on several factors, including household income, where you live while you're studying and what year of study you are in (see Table 10).

If you're living away from home, the maximum loan for English students is £8,700 for the academic year (2018–19), although it's more if you're studying in London. The maximum available is less if you're living with your parents during term time. The costs vary depending on which part of the UK you normally live in and are shown in Table 9 on page 136.

It is vital to remember when considering student loans that both the tuition fee and living expenses loans are not like loans you would get from a bank as you only start paying it back when you have a job that pays over a certain amount. Currently these thresholds are £24,996 per annum (before deductions) for English and Welsh students and £18,330 for Scottish and Northern Irish students. The repayments are then taken directly from your pay packet by your employer.

Table 10 Maximum maintenance loan available (2018–19)

Living arrangements during term time	Maximum maintenance loan available in England	Maximum maintenance loan available in Scotland	Maximum maintenance loan available in Wales	Maximum maintenance loan available in Northern Ireland
Living at home	£7,324	£5,750	£6,650	£3,750
Living away from home and studying outside London	£8,700	£5,750	£8,000	£4,840
Living away from home and studying in London	£11,354	£5,750	£10,250	£6,780

Source: www.gov.uk/student-finance/new-fulltime-students
Contains public sector information licensed under the Open Government Licence v3.0.

Student grants

Historically, the maintenance grant was available to help students with accommodation and other living costs and did not have to be repaid. However, in September 2016, the maintenance grant system was abolished for English students, and as a result, any funding received is now in the form of a loan. Means-tested grants for Scottish, Northern Irish and Welsh students still exist, although this situation may change in the future. The details of grants available are listed below for each country:

England

Most grants have been abolished. Some support may be available to certain students, for example, students with children and students with a disability.

Scotland

Students under the age of 25 may be entitled to the Young Students Bursary (YSB), which is the equivalent of a grant. Currently, if your household income is under £19,000, you receive a maximum of £1,875. This amount then tapers to zero if you have a household income of £34,000 or over per annum. Support may also be available to certain students, for example, lone parents and students with a disability.

Wales

The Welsh Government Learning Grant (WGLG) is a grant available depending on household income. Currently, if household income is less than £18,370 per annum, the maximum amount of £8,100 is payable. This reduces on a sliding scale to a minimum of £1,000 if income exceeds £59,200 per annum.

Additionally, a Special Support Grant (SSG) is available for certain individuals depending on circumstances. For example, this can be paid if you are a single parent, have a disability or are in receipt of certain benefits. For the academic year 2018–19, the maximum is £5,161 per year.

Northern Ireland

Special Support Grants or Maintenance Grants are available in part if household income is less than £41,065. The full grant of £3,475 is awarded if household income is £19,203 or less, and this tapers to zero up to an income of £41,065. Additional support is available to certain students, for example, lone parents and students with a disability.

In all countries where the grant is still available, if your application for a maintenance grant is successful, the value of this will be deducted from your maintenance loan.

NHS bursaries

NHS bursaries are available for students studying their fifth year of dentistry in England, Wales and Northern Ireland, and from the second year onwards for students studying in Scotland. To be eligible for such a bursary, a student must qualify as a home student and be on a 'preregistration health professional training course'. During the first four years of study, dental students are entitled to apply for tuition fee and maintenance loans from Student Finance. From year five onwards, dental students are eligible to apply for a means-tested NHS bursary alongside a reduced student loan to cover maintenance costs. In addition, fees in year five are paid in full by the NHS Student Bursary scheme, though the funding provision varies between England, Wales, Scotland and Northern Ireland. For more information, visit the NHS Health Careers website (www.healthcareers.nhs.uk/career-planning/study-and-training/considering-or-university/financial-support-university).

Scholarships

Certain universities make scholarships available, and these can be a valuable source of income throughout a course. There are some general scholarships as well as ones available only to dentistry students. Details can be obtained from the individual universities, but websites such as www.scholarshiphub.org.uk can provide comprehensive lists of available funding.

In addition to this, the armed forces make scholarships available to students wishing to pursue a career in the medical services. These can be particularly lucrative and will often cover tuition fees as well as paying an annual salary for a part of the course. For example, some cadetships will pay all of your tuition fees, plus an annual salary for your last three years of study and a book allowance. Obviously, this route will not appeal to all students, as it guides you into a career in the armed forces. See page 149 for more details.

10 | What career pathways exist for dentists?

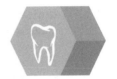

Once you have qualified as a dentist, there are a surprising number of different career pathways that can be followed. This chapter looks at the various options that would be open to you, what each of them entails, and some of the potential advantages and disadvantages of each route.

General dental practitioners (GDPs)

Out of the 41,705 registered dentists in the UK (www.gdc-uk.org/api/files/GDC_Annual_Report_2017.pdf), some will run their own dental practices, while others will work in larger practices or groups of practices. Some will carry out NHS work (24,308 dentists carried out NHS activity in 2017–18) (https://digital.nhs.uk/data-and-information/publications/statistical/nhs-dental-statistics/2017-18-annual-report), while others may take only private patients. Some dental practices will offer both NHS and private treatment. Private patients have a much wider range of treatment available to them, but they or their dental insurance scheme providers pay the full cost – which is determined by the dentist rather than by the NHS. As a result, charges for private dental work can fluctuate widely across the country.

Regardless of these differences, most dentists follow a similar path after graduation. During their final year at dental school, students need to consider where they wish to begin their career. The path chosen will vary depending on the individual student's abilities and interests. Many dental schools organise 'going into practice' days for their students, supplementing information available from the BDA.

Students qualifying at a UK dental school must first complete one year of paid, supervised Dental Foundation Training (DFT) in an approved training practice, but there are also opportunities to carry out another year in an alternative dental setting to provide wider experience. During DFT, the newly graduated dentists (known as Foundation Dentists or FDs) work under supervision in such approved training practices. FDs are paid by the NHS (in 2017–18, they were paid £31,355 per annum), and their trainers are also paid an allowance. Any earnings generated by an FD go to the trainer. Full details of DFT can be found at www.bda. org/students/careers-education/vocational-and-foundation-training. Following DFT, dentists can choose to undertake dental core training or start work in a dental practice. Dental core training lasts between one and three years, and gives the chance to undertake further training in relation to different branches of the world of dentistry before commencing speciality training or starting work as a dentist.

The majority of dentists work as associates. These dentists are self-employed and are responsible for the treatment that they provide, but work in a practice owned by someone else. The associate dentist buys services from the practice owner, such as nursing or technician support, materials and access to patients, paying the practice owner either a percentage of their earnings or a fixed monthly fee.

At a later point in their career, many dentists decide to acquire their own practice. They can do so by buying an existing practice, starting a brand new practice or becoming a partner in an existing practice. Whichever they opt for, it ultimately means they are self-employed and involved in running a small business. In addition to being dentists they are thus also business people and are responsible not only for the treatment that they provide for their own patients but also for the administration of the practice, and the employment of associate dentists if necessary. This element of a career in dentistry can be an attractive proposition, as it allows a love of dentistry and a flair for business to be developed side by side; however, there can be greater stresses and risks associated with following this path.

A very important aspect of a career in dentistry is the ongoing professional development that takes place; a dentist is responsible for structuring and developing their career at their own pace and in the direction they wish. This means that a dentist is always learning and seeking to develop new skills and knowledge in their profession. Currently, the requirement for dentists is to carry out 100 hours of verifiable continuous professional development (CPD) every five years, with the requirement to declare at least 10 hours in any two-year period.

As with medical general practitioners, GDPs have the opportunity to form long-term relationships with their patients and provide them with continuing care. This means that a dentist can develop long-term community links and make a real difference to the area where they are based.

Case study: Dr Kully Shoker, studied at King's College, University of London

'I qualified from King's in 1998 and then spent two years in a General Professional Training post at Newcastle Dental Hospital. This involved part time in a hospital post and part time in practice – this incorporated the initial Foundation Training position required to allow independent working practice in England. During this time I undertook a Diploma in Conscious Sedation and my diploma with the Royal College of Physicians and Surgeons, Glasgow (MFDS RCPS). I returned to work in the West Midlands in 2001 into full time general practice. During this time I undertook a Master of Philosophy degree – this was a research degree into endodontic practice in general practice. I am currently undertaking another master's degree at the University of Birmingham.

'I purchased my own practice in 2003 and currently still work there with four other dentists and a hygienist. A majority of our work is provided on the NHS and a limited amount privately. My other role is that I am a Programme Director for Foundation Training, with Health Education England. This is a role that involves helping train dentists who are just out of dental school and just graduated. I am also a Mentor with Health Education England in the West Midlands and also examine for the Royal College of Surgeons, England.

'I currently work in a very busy practice. We have a team of 19 people and carry out a wide range of dentistry on a well-established patient base of approximately 15,000 patients. All the dentists are carrying out postgraduate studies, demonstrating their commitment to lifelong learning. We are also a Foundation Training practice, so each year we have a trainee to look after.

'There are several aspects of being a dentist that I find immensely rewarding. First of all, the contact with patients and getting to know them over the years is a delight. I have been at the same practice for over 13 years now so have well-established relationships with many of my patients. Not only is it a great ice-breaker when they walk into the surgery, especially if they are nervous about having some dental treatment, but it allows all sides to understand we are dealing with human beings and the care and compassion that needs to be shown. It is not just a "consumer" relationship.

'Equally, there is a reciprocal relationship, where patients have taken great interest in what I like to do outside of the dental surgery and ask questions about my own family.

'Second, the challenge of helping a patient, especially one who may have had a problem for some time or been in considerable pain. Knowing you possess the skills to help detect, diagnose and treat provides a very fulfilling feeling. The job is very technical and most dentists will agree that we continue to strive each year to improve our skills through experience, working with peers and undertaking extensive postgraduate studies and courses.

'Third, working closely with a team of like-minded people. General practice, where I am based, is a fantastic opportunity to craft a team of individuals who work well as a team with a common goal. Ultimately, you become like a little family. Which means you do have ups and downs but generally your common goal unites you, which in this case, is to strive to provide exceptional care to our patients. Patients will often comment in our surveys how impressed they have been with the reception team or a particular nurse. Funnily, you don't often find them commenting too much on the dentistry, unless some issues arose. This does demonstrate how much emphasis patients put on all the "peripheral" things outside of the technical aspect of dentistry and why it is important to keep a keen eye on these as well as just the technical side of the job.

'My final point is that the job itself allows individuals to use many skills. Not only are you undertaking a hands-on job, but you are also using the skills of an excellent communicator, a great leader, someone who can inspire a team and be self-motivated. There are such a wide range of career pathways in dentistry, which often undergraduates are not aware of until they qualify. So the world really can be their oyster if they wish!

'Dentistry is a great career, but as with every job, it can come with significant challenges; contractual changes have provided such challenges in recent years. Whereby medical colleagues' challenges have been highlighted significantly in the press, dentistry does not get the same exposure.

'We are in an era where funding needs to be carefully monitored and value for money is high on the agenda for any government. There is an increasing number of litigious cases in dentistry in the UK. These stem for a variety of reasons. Therefore, as a professional, dentists are probably more careful and even nervous about treatment delivery than they have ever been. This can make the job very stressful. It also can influence how treatment is offered to patients. This balancing act is probably at the foremost of a majority of NHS dentists' minds currently.

'Over the last decade or so, the amount of external regulation has also increased immensely. Though this itself is not seen as an issue per se, especially as any profession should be open to inspection and scrutiny by external bodies, to demonstrate quality control is in place, the level of inspection does not always equate to a "good" or "bad" practice. The administrative burden of running a practice is enormous, so those that own practices have to spend a considerable amount of their time involved in this, as well as needing an outstanding team to help and delegate to. This can be a big distraction from the delivery of care to patients, though aspects of it are integral to experience.

'The costs of training postgraduate dentists are also very high. There is a lot of motivation amongst dentists to enhance their skills and for some they may wish to specialise in a particular field. The costs involved in this require careful personal planning, as it will have a considerable impact. For some, this may mean a delay in considering buying a house, getting married, starting a family etc. So it is not always a straightforward journey to embark on. As dentists leave university with a lot of student debt, due to the length of the course, this additional financial burden can take a long time to repay.

'One of the most important tips for aspiring dentists is "understand people" and "understand yourself". The focus for most students is academic, as ultimately, it is the grades that will get you to university. However, skills in surgery and dentistry are motor skills, and can be taught to most, if not all, with enough time and practice. What can be more of a challenge is the communication skills required. Some have these as natural attributes, others not! Anyone wishing to work with patients needs to prioritise their skills in this area. Some understanding of psychology would also be useful – even consider it as an A-level option. Again this will be useful in daily practice when dealing directly with patients.'

Hospital and community dentists

Hospital dentistry

Hospital dentistry concentrates on more specialist areas such as orthodontics, restorative dentistry for victims of accidents or illness, paediatric dentistry or oral medicine. As a hospital dentist, the career path is similar to that followed by a doctor: junior, specialty and so on, up to consultant level.

Unlike GDPs, hospital dentists receive a salary. Hospital dentistry is thus possibly less risky, as it is salaried, full-time. Hospital dentists generally work as part of a team, have access to specialised diagnostic facilities and work with consultants in other specialisations. Another advantage is that, in the hospital service, there is a prescribed and well-defined career structure and training pathway. However, the hours are not as flexible and time will be spent 'on call', potentially resulting in long working sessions.

Community Dental Services

Some newly qualified dentists prefer to follow a more structured path, and choose to become part of the Community Dental Services, which provide dental treatment to a wide range of vulnerable patients. This includes providing treatment in a community setting for patients who, for whatever reason, cannot visit their local GDP. This type of treatment is commonly provided to housebound people, people with mental health problems or other disabilities and vulnerable patients. Within this area, there are often opportunities to undertake research and be involved in studies in relation to epidemiology and public health.

As with the hospital service, these posts are salaried and there is a career structure, but this option is less structured than working in the hospital setting. It is possible to carry out your DFT in the Community Dental Service.

Dental specialisms

There are a wide range of specialities that exist in the world of dentistry which can have a great impact on where you work and what you do on a day-to-day basis. Any dentist can work in any field, but only those on the GDC specialist lists can class themselves as a 'specialist'.

The GDC maintains a register of dentists who are entitled to use the title of specialist in relation to any of the 13 areas of specialisation. Dentists can only use the title specialist if they have completed a GDC approved programme in that particular area and have been awarded a Certificate of Completion of Specialist Training (CCST). Once these criteria have been met, the dentist will be added to the GDC list of specialists. Dentists are under no obligation to specialise, although, in the long term, specialisation can enhance career prospects and earnings, particularly in specialisms related to cosmetic dentistry.

The following sections briefly look at the major specialisations in dentistry as outlined by the GDC. Further information on specialisms can be found at www.gdc-uk.org/patients/look-for-a-specialist.

Special care dentistry

This specialism relates to the improvement of the oral health of adolescents and adults who have some form of impairment or disability.

Oral surgery

Oral surgery is used to correct a wide spectrum of diseases, injuries and defects in the jaw and mouth. This is a slightly more intrusive form of surgery than typical root canal or cavity fillings. It usually requires the use of anaesthetic and therefore patients take longer to recover.

Examples of oral surgery include having wisdom teeth removed and getting dental implants.

Orthodontics

Orthodontics is a specialty of dentistry that is centred on the study and treatment of malocclusions (improper bites), which may result in tooth irregularity, out-of-proportion jaw relationships, or both. Orthodontic correction has a very positive effect on facial appearance.

Paediatric dentistry

Paediatric dentistry is the practice and teaching of and research into oral healthcare for children from birth to adolescence. Children are unique in their stages of development, oral disease and oral health needs, which is why paediatric dentistry covers all aspects of their oral healthcare. It aims to improve oral health in children and encourage the highest standards of clinical care.

Endodontics

Endodontics deals with the health, injuries and diseases of the pulp and periradicular region (the tooth root and its surrounding tissue), such as root canal injuries, which can harm the nervous system as well.

Periodontics

Periodontics deals with the supporting structures of teeth; it includes the treatment of patients with severe gum disease.

Prosthodontics

Prosthodontics deals mainly with the replacement of hard and soft tissues using crowns, bridges, dentures and implants. It focuses on treatment planning, rehabilitation and maintenance of the oral function, comfort and appearance.

Restorative dentistry

Restorative dentistry is the study, diagnosis and effective management of diseases of the teeth and their supporting structures. It includes endodontics, periodontics and prosthodontics.

Dental public health

Dental public health is a non-clinical specialty that includes assessment of dental health needs and ensuring that dental services meet those needs. It is mainly concerned with improving the dental health of a population rather than that of individuals and involves working in primary care trusts, government offices and strategic health authorities. There are a few such academic posts in universities and in the Department of Health.

Oral medicine

This is concerned with the diagnosis and non-surgical management of medical pathology affecting the oral area, jaw and face. Many oral medicine specialists have dual qualifications, with both medical and dental degrees. The main aspects of oral medicine are clinical care, research and undergraduate and postgraduate teaching.

Oral microbiology

This is the study of the diverse and complex microbial community in the mouth and is carried out by laboratory-based professionals. The primary role of an oral microbiologist is to diagnose bacterial and fungal infections in the head and mouth.

Oral and maxillofacial pathology

Oral and maxillofacial pathology is the branch of dentistry concerned with diseases of oral structures, including soft tissues, teeth, jaws and salivary glands. It is a science that investigates the causes, processes and effects of these diseases. The practice of oral pathology includes research into and diagnosis of diseases using clinical, radiographic and biochemical means.

Dental and maxillofacial radiology

Dental and maxillofacial radiology involves a combination of radiology and dentistry. It is mainly concerned with using and understanding the diagnostic imaging modalities that are used in dentistry.

Other careers in dentistry

In addition to the common career paths outlined above, dentists can also find employment in the armed forces and industry. For those with an interest in the academic aspects of dentistry, there are also opportunities for research or teaching in universities; some dentists will opt to become teachers or lecturers in dental schools and involved in research.

Dental bodies corporate (DBCs)

Corporations that can practise dentistry in the UK are known as dental bodies corporate. There is now no limit on the number of DBCs that can exist.

By law, DBCs have to be registered with the GDC. This sector is currently on the increase, due to a general move away from NHS dentistry, a growing consumerism among the general public (e.g. wealthier patients demanding top-notch care) and deregulation of the profession, allowing dentists to advertise, thus making company branding possible. A further reason given by the BDA is the belief of venture capitalists, among others, that investment in dentistry will yield attractive returns.

Dentistry in the armed forces

All three defence forces employ dentists to provide a comprehensive service for personnel, both abroad and in the UK. Dentists hold a commissioned rank and there is a very structured career path to follow. One of the possible benefits of following this route is that financial scholarships may be available during your studies. It is also possible to carry out DFT in this sector. For more information on careers in armed forces dentistry, visit the army's website and the Defence Medical Services' website, provided by the Ministry of Defence:

- www.army.mod.uk/medical-services/dental.aspx
- www.gov.uk/government/groups/defence-medical-services.

Dentistry in industry

Some large manufacturing and engineering companies (e.g. oil companies and car manufacturers) offer dental services to their employees. These posts are salaried but the role is equivalent to that of a GDP.

University teaching and research

If you like both teaching and research at university level, there are opportunities in this field. Careers in university dental schools allow you to specialise in a particular aspect of dentistry, which can enable you to pursue research into a specific interest in great depth. University dental teachers will have gained postgraduate qualifications and can progress to become senior lecturers or professors and, if they so wish, get involved with writing teaching materials.

Running a business

Running a dental practice involves all of the skills required in running a business as well as the skills needed to be a dentist. This means that a practice will have to rent or buy a site, employ qualified staff, train them, pay tax and so on. The income of a practice serves to pay the employees, rates and rent. A proportion of the profit is reinvested in the practice for new equipment or new facilities, so that it can continue to offer the best service to its patients. Dentists will be managing a team of people encompassing dental nurses, hygienists, receptionists and others, so good administrative and managerial abilities are needed.

Running a practice can potentially be lucrative, but there are a number of factors that must be considered carefully. These are things such as working long hours, stress and frustrations with the NHS – all of which can be disheartening and unpleasant for a dentist to deal with.

The wider team

Being a dentist in any setting is not just about working on your own carrying out dental treatments; a vital part is working within a team made up of numerous different members. The people who work most closely with dentists are dental nurses, dental hygienists and receptionists or administrative staff. The point of mentioning these team members is to raise awareness of some of the important people that you will need to find, employ and train as a practice partner or owner.

Dental nurses

Perhaps the most important person as far as the dentist is concerned is the dental nurse, who plays a key role in any dental practice. Working alongside the dentist, it is the nurse's job to provide a high standard of care for patients and to be the dentist's assistant. They provide skilled supportive care and are able to perform diagnostic tests such as X-rays.

Dental hygienists

The dental hygienist is also a very important part of the dental team. They are licensed dental professionals with a degree specialising in preventive dental care and focusing on techniques in oral hygiene. In most cases, the hygienist is employed by a dental practice. Procedures performed by hygienists include cleaning, scaling, radiography and dental sealing.

Receptionists and administration staff

The first person you will encounter when you telephone or visit a dental practice is the receptionist. The receptionist is there to manage patients' bookings. In practices where there are multiple practitioners, efficient and effective administrative staff are crucial to the viability and long-term profit and health of the practice. In taking care of the appointments process and correspondence at a busy practice, they allow dentists more time to focus on their work.

Salaries and wages

According to Prospects Career Planner (www.prospects.ac.uk/job-profiles/dentist) a typical starting salary for a dentist during their foundation training year is £31,355 (November 2018 figure). This is expected to increase significantly over the career of a dentist, but the amount by which it increases will depend on the career path that a dentist chooses. In a report released in August 2018, NHS Digital gave details of the average earnings of different types of dentists in both NHS and private settings. The overall average gross earning of an associate dentist was £106,400 per annum, with a providing-performer (one who has contracts with local health bodies) earning an average of £381,200. Note that these figures apply to England and Wales.

Before you begin to think about what you could buy when you start earning these amounts, you should be aware that the expenses associated with running a practice (for instance, wages, materials and the practice building) can take a large portion of this income; the average percentage of earnings spent for all self-employed dentists in the 2016/17 financial year was 52.9%. (Source: https://files.digital.nhs.uk/7C/0270BAdent-earn-expe-2016-17-rep%20v1.1.pdf.)

A dentist who opts to work in a salaried post in the Community Dental Service can expect to earn between £38,861 and £83,118 (November 2018). Other salaried posts exist in the armed forces and in corporate practices. In NHS hospitals, salaries at the consultant level range from £76,761 to £103,490 (November 2018). (Source: www.healthcareers.nhs.uk/explore-roles/dental-team/roles-dental-team/dentist/pay-dentists.)

It is not surprising that, in the private sector, providing-performer dentists earned £184,000 on average in 2016–17 after expenses. This can, of course, be far greater, depending on the type of dental practice and the amount of work a dentist is prepared to do. For instance, surgical and cosmetic dentistry are two areas that command the high-end costs in the market.

One factor to consider is that, unlike other careers where earnings rise year after year, dentists often reach a peak in their thirties, and their earnings can fall after this as they become older, slower and less inclined to work long hours.

Case study: Anthony Dash, studied at the University of Birmingham

'I qualified as a dentist in 1988 and started working in an NHS practice in 1989. I went on to buy the business in 1990 and by 1995 had grown it to include five practices. I then subsequently sold the NHS practices so that I could focus on providing high quality private dental services to patients.

'My current place of work focuses on cosmetic dentistry, which is a highly rewarding specialism. This can be extremely demanding due to the high expectations that our patients have, but is also hugely fulfilling when we provide this to them.

'The most satisfying element of my job is when we are able to surpass expectations with the quality of work we provide. We aim to improve our patients' oral health, make them proud to smile again and achieve all this in a relaxed, non-invasive and painless way.

'Overall, I find being a dentist extremely satisfying, but dealing with people and their personalities can prove challenging at times. This includes staff as much as patients at times.

'The field of dentistry is always evolving and, in my opinion, one of the most topical areas in cosmetic dentistry is providing treatment with the minimum invasiveness, for example the use of short-term orthodontics such as 'Invisalign' invisible braces to straighten and whiten teeth. Tooth whitening systems and cosmetic smile make-overs are also topical at the moment.

'I would really recommend this vocation to all aspiring dentists. It's a fantastic profession to enter into at the moment with so many new innovations. However, the work needed to graduate is excessive and anyone thinking about applying for dentistry must be totally committed if they are going to succeed.'

Graduate prospects

In a recent study published in April 2017, the Department for Education found that in 2017, 88.7% of young graduates (aged 21–30) were employed (https://assets.publishing.service.gov.uk/government/uploads/system/uploads/attachment_data/file/701720/GLMS_2017.pdf). As with any vocation, it it is worth considering whether a dentistry degree will be an asset or a liability in the job market of the future, and what the prospects are for successfully entering employment following the completion of your dental degree and training.

The *Guardian*'s online university guide (www.guardian.co.uk/education/universityguide) gives data on the number of graduates from each dental school being employed six months after graduation. The general picture here is that the job market for dentists remains buoyant and there is still strong demand, and indeed a very high probability of being employed soon after finishing your education. The percentage of graduates in graduate-level employment after six months ranges from 96.5% to 100%, with an average employment rate of 98.9%, so job prospects are outstanding when compared to other graduates. Even more reassuring is that there are three dental schools reporting a 100% success rate. This is an amazing statistic and provides a real insight into the employment prospects that this vocation can provide.

At this point in time and for the foreseeable future, it seems that a dentistry degree will represent a solid investment and lead to excellent job prospects following graduation. At a time when some graduates can really struggle to find work, this potentially makes studying dentistry an even more attractive proposition than it already was.

Case study: Sameera Mukadam, just entered employment

'I studied at the University of Manchester and have just started my first job as a General Dental Practitioner. I really enjoyed my time at Manchester and feel that the course was excellent preparation for the world of work.

'Manchester has a focus on early clinical contact, so in my first year, I was meeting patients along with my clinical partner and by my second year I was experiencing my first proper patient contact. I feel that the early exposure is really important and helped me to understand the demands of working with people. On reflection, I found the best bits of the course to be related to meeting patients and ultimately having the independence to devise and implement a treatment plan. However, it can be pot luck as to which patients you get to treat and this can sometimes lead to dealing with lots of simple cases with lots of repetition.

'When starting my degree, it was a bit of a culture shock compared to A levels; it can be a real challenge when you don't know how much you need to know to meet the demands of the course. Many students also struggle with the time demands of the course and the way it will inevitably impact on your life.

'The vast majority of patients are really enjoyable to work with, but everyone gets some that can be difficult. In third year, I was treating a schizophrenic patient who kept yanking the drill out of their mouth when being treated. Ultimately, I had to simplify my communication with the patient and use techniques that I would usually employ when treating a child. I also had a patient that kept changing their mind about the treatment and again had to go back to basics in terms of communicating the details of the procedure again and again.

'As a dentist, I love the chance I have to develop relationships with patients over a long period of time and find positive feedback

---

from them when they are happy with the work you have completed to be particularly rewarding; I will always remember a patient that bought me a hot water bottle as a thank you gift as I was always saying I was cold!

'In my opinion, one of the key issues related to dentistry is the cost of treatment. Patients will often complain about how much it can cost for complex procedures. The threat of patients taking legal action against a dentist is also a potential challenge. We were taught at university that it will happen at least once in each dentist's career, so it is important to have the appropriate insurance and make use of the advice and support available.

'My tips for aspiring dentists are as follows:

- stay on top of your workload; organising yourself is key to success
- don't leave things until the last minute
- be friendly with everyone on your course, you never know who you will have to work with as a clinical partner!
- have other interests outside of your course; balancing extra-curricular interests with work is important for your sanity
- enjoy it while you can; your time at university is over very quickly!'

11 | Further information

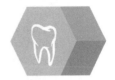

Further reading

There is a wealth of information available both on the internet and beyond. Try to keep up to date with some of the key developments as this will give you an excellent overview of what is happening in the world of dentistry.

An essential starting point is the BDA's website (www.bda.org). This carries careers information for prospective dentists as well as press releases and discussion of topical issues.

The BDA has its own museum, the BDA Dental Museum, which gives an interesting historical overview of dentistry; details can be found at www.bda.org/museum. Some other useful websites are www.dentistry. co.uk, www.dentalhealth.org, www.gdc-uk.org and www.the-dentist. co.uk. These all have a wealth of factual information and details of current affairs relating to dentistry and as such are worth a regular look. www.thestudentroom.co.uk is a chat room for potential students and has a number of interesting discussions relating to dental admissions; however, double check any information you receive from here as it may not always be reliable.

All university websites have a wealth of information about entrance requirements and this should be used as your primary source of information for questions about admissions. The UCAS website (www.ucas. com) also pulls together summaries of the key admissions information.

The BDA publishes a journal for dentists, the *British Dental Journal* (www.nature.com/bdj). The journal is aimed at practising dentists and can be very technical, although it does give very good short summaries of some of the most relevant hot topics.

To keep up to date with dentistry and dental issues in the UK, the *Independent*, the *Guardian*, the *Daily Telegraph* and *The Times* all carry regular health reporting and have health sections once a week.

For summaries of course information and academic requirements, a useful reference point is *HEAP 2020 University Degree Course Offers*, written by Brian Heap and published by Trotman (www.trotman.co.uk).

Organisations

British Dental Association
64 Wimpole Street
London W1G 8YS
www.bda.org
Tel: 020 7935 0875
Email: enquiries@bda.org,uk

British Fluoridation Society
PO Box 731
Oldham OL1 9PH
www.bfsweb.org
Tel: 07947 613062
Email: info@bfsweb.org

British Medical Association
BMA House
Tavistock Square
London WC1H 9JP
www.bma.org.uk
Tel: 020 7387 4499

General Dental Council
37 Wimpole Street
London W1G 8DQ
www.gdc-uk.org
Tel: 020 7167 6000

Dental schools

University of Aberdeen
Institute of Dentistry
Cornhill Rd
Aberdeen AB25 2ZR
www.abdn.ac.uk/dental/
Email: dentistry@abdn.ac.uk

University of Birmingham
Birmingham Dental Hospital and School of Dentistry
5 Mill Pool Way
Birmingham B5 7EG
www.birmingham.ac.uk/schools/dentistry
Tel: 0121 466 5472

University of Bristol
Bristol Dental School
Lower Maudlin Street
Bristol BS1 2LY
www.bristol.ac.uk/dental
Tel: 0117 394 1649
Email: choosebristol-ug@bristol.ac.uk

Cardiff University
Dental School
University Hospital Wales
Heath Park
Cardiff CF14 4XY

www.cardiff.ac.uk/dentistry
Tel: 029 2074 2468/6917
Email: dentalugadmissions@cardiff.ac.uk

University of Central Lancashire
The School of Dentistry
University of Central Lancashire
Preston
Lancashire PR1 2HE
www.uclan.ac.uk/schools/dentistry/index.php
Tel: 01772 892400
Email: cenquiries@uclan.ac.uk

University of Dundee
Dundee Dental School
University of Dundee
Park Place
Dundee DD1 4HN
www.dentistry.dundee.ac.uk
Tel: 01382 381600
Email: asrs-dentistry@dundee.ac.uk

University of Glasgow
Glasgow Dental Hospital and School
378 Sauchiehall Street
Glasgow G2 3JZ
www.gla.ac.uk/schools/dental
Tel: 0141 211 9703
Email: med-sch-dental-ug@glasgow.ac.uk

King's College London
Guy's Campus
King's College London Dental Institute
Faculty Office, Floor 18, Guy's Tower
Guy's Hospital
London SE1 9RT
www.kcl.ac.uk/dentistry
Tel: 020 7188 7188
Denmark Hill Campus
King's College London Dental Institute
Bessemer Road
Denmark Hill
London SE5 9RW
Tel: 020 3299 9000
www.kcl.ac.uk/dentistry

University of Leeds
School of Dentistry
Leeds Dental Institute
Clarendon Way
Leeds LS2 9LU
https://medhealth.leeds.ac.uk/dentistry
Tel: 0113 343 9922
Email: denadmissions@leeds.ac.uk

University of Liverpool
School of Dentistry
University of Liverpool
Pembroke Place
Liverpool L3 5PS
www.liverpool.ac.uk/dentistry
Tel: 0151 706 5298
Email: dentenq@liverpool.ac.uk

University of Manchester
Faculty of Biology, Medicine and Health
The University of Manchester
Oxford Road
Manchester M13 9PL
www.bmh.manchester.ac.uk/dentistry/
Tel: 0161 306 0211
Email: ug.dentistry@manchester.ac.uk

Newcastle University
School of Dental Sciences
Newcastle University
Framlington Place
Newcastle upon Tyne NE2 4BW
www.ncl.ac.uk/dental
Tel: 0191 208 8245

Plymouth University
Drake Circus
Plymouth
Devon
PL4 8AA
www.plymouth.ac.uk/schools/peninsula-school-of-dentistry
Tel: 01752 437333
Email: meddent-admissions@plymouth.ac.uk

Queen Mary (Barts and The London School of Medicine and Dentistry)

Barts and The London School of Medicine and Dentistry
Queen Mary University of London
Turner Street
London E1 2AD
www.dentistry.qmul.ac.uk
Tel: 020 7882 2240
Email: dentistry@qmul.ac.uk

Queen's University Belfast

School of Medicine, Dentistry and Biomedical Sciences
Queen's University Belfast
97 Lisburn Rd
Belfast BT9 7BL
www.qub.ac.uk/schools/mdbs/dentistry
Tel: 028 9097 2215

University of Sheffield

The School of Clinical Dentistry
University of Sheffield
19 Claremont Crescent
Sheffield S10 2TA
www.sheffield.ac.uk/dentalschool/index
Tel: 0114 215 9307
Email: dental.admissions@sheffield.ac.uk

Glossary

Associate dentists
Dentists who are self-employed and are responsible for the treatment that they provide, but work in a practice owned by someone else.

Bachelor of Dental Surgery (BDS)
The degree you will be awarded from most universities upon completion of your dental degree.

BChD
The same as BDS, but the Latin equivalent.

BioMedical Admissions Test (BMAT)
A pre-admissions test used currently by the University of Leeds to distinguish between applicants.

British Dental Association (BDA)
A professional association and trade union for dentists in the United Kingdom.

Clearing
The system whereby students can gain entry to a university course in the period after results are released if they have not achieved the required grades.

Community Dental Services
The service in the UK that is currently responsible for the treatment of people with special medical or social needs, such as complex medical problems, disabilities or mental health problems, who are unable to be treated by general dental practitioners (GDPs).

Continuous professional development (CPD)
The ongoing training that a dentist must complete throughout their career. A dentist must complete a specified amount each year.

Dental Foundation Training (DFT)
The one-year period of training carried out by dentists following graduation.

Endodontics
A dental specialism related to the health of the tooth root and its surrounding tissue.

Fluoride
A group of inorganic fluorine-containing compounds found in water supplies and toothpastes which reduce tooth decay.

General dental practitioner (GDP)
A dentist who provides general dental care to the public either privately or through the NHS.

IELTS
The International English Language Testing System. Students who do not have English as their first language must reach a certain IELTS level in order to gain entry to study dentistry.

Intercalated BSc
At some universities it is possible to take an additional year to complete an intercalated degree. This results in obtaining an extra BSc in addition to the BDS qualification you will receive at the end of the dentistry course.

Multiple mini interviews (MMIs)
An alternative interview format that requires interviewees to move between numerous stations to answer questions.

Orthodontics
A dental specialism involved with the treatment of improper bites.

Overseas Registration Exam (ORE)
Currently, students who complete a dental degree outside the European Economic Area (EEA) are required to complete this exam prior to becoming a registered dentist in this country.

Paediatric dentistry
A specialism related to working with children.

Periodontics
A specialism dealing with the supporting structures of teeth.

Problem-based learning (PBL)
A style of teaching used by some dental schools that relies heavily on independent study.

Prosthodontics
A dental specialism dealing with the replacement of hard and soft tissues using crowns, bridges, dentures and implants.

Self-directed learning
A style of learning where the student takes responsibility for their direction of study and the study they undertake.

UCAS
The Universities and Colleges Admissions Service. Your application will be made through this service.

The University Clinical Aptitude Test (UCAT)
A pre-admissions test used by most dental schools to distinguish between applicants.

Vocational dental practitioners (VDP)
Graduate dentists who are undertaking their vocational training are known as VDPs.